☆ ☆

Celebrity Stew

☆ ☆

Celebrity Stew

By

Leo Pearlstein

Food Publicity
Pioneer Shares
50 Years of Entertaining
Inside Stories of
Hollywood Royalty

Foreword By
Steve Allen

Hollywood Circle Press
Los Angeles

Celebrity Stew

HOLLYWOOD CIRCLE PRESS

P.O. Box 48051
Los Angeles, CA 90048
Website: www.celebritystew.com

This book is available through most bookstores or directly from the publisher at the above address or website.

Printed and bound in the United States of America

Celebrity Stew
Copyright 2003 By Leo Pearlstein
Library of Congress Control Number 2001092492
First Edition
ISBN 0-9711306-0-4

Design by Bill Goldfine, Los Angeles, CA

☆ ☆

To my family, especially my wife, Helen, who helped me begin my business over 50 years ago and continues to be my greatest inspiration.

Featured on the cover:

(clockwise from top left)
Bob Hope
Mickey Rooney
Phyllis Diller
Jimmy Durante
Abbott(r.) & Costello
Wayne Newton, Karen Lindsey
John F. Kennedy
Steve Allen (cntr.)

Contents

☆ ☆

☆ ☆

Celebrity Stew

☆ ☆

Other books by
Leo Pearlstein,
"Recipes Of The Stars"

Acknowledgements

☆ ☆

My sincere thanks to the many people who helped me make this book possible: Lisa Messinger, a food editor with The Copley National Newspaper Syndicate, who encouraged me to write the book after she wrote the feature about me entitled, "Mr. Food"; entertainer, comedian, actor, composer and author, the late Steve Allen, who encouraged and counseled me, and wrote the Foreword; Donna Larsen, who did a fantastic job of editing all of the material with the support of Howard Pearlstein, who spent countless hours working with Donna and me to put all of my stories together and help structure the book; and Bill Goldfine, who supervised the creative production and helped immensely with putting the book into its finished form.

Many thanks to Helen Pearlstein, Frank Pearlstein, David Pearlstein, and Karen Lindsey Jackson, who spent many hours reviewing a mountain of material and photos, and also to Jacqueline Madarang and Rachelle Bugtong for their tireless efforts as my ever-ready word processing wizards.

Thanks to several of my very good friends, old and new, some who gave me advice and some who reminded me of my most entertaining publicity events: Art Silver, Joe Bardo, James Bacon, Fran Giedt, Bob Barker, Paul Durbin, Dotti Bernhard, Marcie Rothman, Vern Lanegrasse, Francine York, Irwin Zucker, Marj Walker, Seymour Cohen, Steve Blackman, Jeff Kasmer, Joann Killeen and Pete Masterson.

Last, but certainly not least, deepest thanks to actor Eddie Bracken, who encouraged me to begin my career and opened the door to my adventures in celebrity publicity.

LEO PEARLSTEIN

Foreword

☆ ☆

Leo Pearlstein is one of the pioneers of good, old-fashioned publicity. This book is full of examples of how Leo and his staff were able to publicize their clients' products in clever ways, using popular film and TV stars. It also shows the creativity and coordination of well-planned special events and publicity stunts. These public relations and publicity activities are just as practical today as when Leo created them years ago.

One is impressed to see so many photos of stars like Bob Hope, Jack Benny, Bing Crosby, Dinah Shore, Bill Cosby, Tony Curtis and Janet Leigh, James Mason, Abbott & Costello, Danny Thomas, Groucho Marx, Don Knotts, George Foreman, Wayne Newton, Rock Hudson, Buddy Hackett, Phyllis Diller, Walter Mathau, George Burns and Gracie Allen, Lloyd Bridges with his sons, Beau and Jeff, as well as Mickey Rooney, Liberace, Jayne Mansfield, Steve Lawrence and Eydie Gormé, Jimmy Stewart, Lucille Ball and others. They all had something to do with Leo's clients' products and each has a different story.

The book offers a fresh take on Hollywood nostalgia. In addition to Leo's comments and philosophies on each of the adventures he shares, the book is a lesson in solid public relations, while also being quite entertaining.

I met Leo over 40 years ago as he was publicizing various food industries. The guests he produced were young, attractive women with such titles as Miss Turkey Stuffing, Miss Boysenberry, Miss Cranberry, Miss Chive and Miss Apple. All were extremely knowledgeable about the commodity they represented and were also entertaining and informative.

We would set up elaborate sketches, at times having me change into an appropriate costume. For example, when Leo arranged for Miss Apple to appear on our show, we created a Garden of Eden theme on stage. She came out in a green, leafy bathing suit and my staff surrounded me on stage while I changed into a leopard-skin caveman outfit. "Eve" fed me a variety of apple-related products.

On another show, Miss Boysenberry gave us a wealth of information. I don't think the audience really knew that much about the product. In addition to telling us that boysenberries were developed by Rudolf Boysen back in 1923, and offering information about where they are grown, she had an elaborate presentation of boysenberry products, including jam, jelly, pancake syrup, tarts and cookies, as well as boysenberry brandy, wine, sherbet, and ice cream.

She even had our band play a song written especially for my show, which she sang, called "The Boysenberry Jam." We both danced, kind of a twist, and the audience went wild.

While my purpose in having these guests appear on my show with their products was to entertain our viewers, as well as educate them, Leo's purpose was to get positive exposure for his clients' products.

Read the book, laugh and learn something about public relations and publicity from Leo Pearlstein's always creative approach.

STEVE ALLEN (1921-2000)

Steve in Eden with "Miss Apple" (Louise Lawson).

The King of Culinary Public Relations

☆ ☆

In 2000, Leo Pearlstein celebrated his 50th anniversary in the public relations business. He has spent a half-century known to many as the nation's unofficial "king of culinary public relations," a niche he pioneered and of which he and two of his sons are still on the cutting edge. He is the consummate behind-the-scenes man who helped create many of the most interesting and uproarious segments on talk-show television. He has also created publicity opportunities with many of the film industry's favorite stars. That is why he has written this book, to share with you—the reader—his many adventures, and misadventures, in promoting food products among famous people. In fact, sometimes the food—be it chives, prunes or boysenberries—upstaged the stars.

Leo practicing what he preaches (early 1950's)

It all started with a star, Eddie Bracken, one of the film greats of the 1940s ("Hail the Conquering Hero" and "The Miracle of Morgan's Creek") who also owned the Jenkins & Large Advertising Agency and Bracken Television Productions. (How many Hollywood trivia buffs out there know that Bracken was also in advertising?) One of Bracken's vice presidents had just hired 27-year-old Leo Pearlstein in 1947. Having worked briefly in sales at Hunt-Wesson Foods, Leo immediately made a mark by bringing in Jenkins & Large's first food accounts. "You could tell right away that there was something special about Leo,"

Eddie Bracken—(in 2000)
a star forever

☆ ☆

Bracken said in an interview 50 years later.

Leo Pearlstein, who had been an award-winning student in one of the first classes of marketing students ever to be graduated from the University of Southern California, had helped run his parents' Los Angeles grocery market. Leo, from a very young age, was destined to educate the public about food. Early in his career, he produced one of the first frozen food commercials, featuring Wong's Chinese Food Company—for television, which was still in its infant stages.

While working with Eddie Bracken, Leo noticed that this celebrity was not only a major player in films, but worked regularly with other big stars who posed for his advertising campaigns. Although busy with his food accounts, Leo's observations concerning the show biz area of the business would later help him create a unique place for himself in culinary public relations, one that he has successfully maintained for over 50 years.

In 1950, Eddie Bracken decided to close Jenkins & Large. "I said something to Leo like, 'Go forth, young man, and make a big mark with your own company. Take all the food accounts with my blessing,'" Bracken recalled. That is when Lee & Associates, Inc. sprang to life. Sometimes fate kicks you out on your own before you think you're ready, but Leo had the vision to make it work. The excitement of having his own public relations firm outweighed his nervousness at venturing out on his own. Leo rented a tiny, one-room office near the historic Farmer's Market on Fairfax Avenue in Los Angeles. He certainly couldn't have picked a better locale for generating food publicity!

Lee & Associates, Inc., specializing in both public relations and advertising, was founded by Leo Pearlstein and his wife Helen, in 1950. As Leo was called "Lee" by his friends, he continued under that name. The company consisted of one part-time secretary, two part-time artists, a copywriter, a consultant, and a student intern in advertising from the University of Southern California. From that day forward, Leo has approached the stars about posing with food products made by his wide variety of culinary clientele. "People often ask me how I got someone like Groucho Marx to pose with California Long White potatoes, or Dragnet's Jack Webb to pose with a turkey or prunes, or Bing Crosby, carving a turkey or posing with a musket and wearing a pilgrim's hat with a Thanksgiving turkey," Leo said. "I made it work because I could see from early on in my career that this would give them a much wider area of publicity than they could otherwise get in the traditional entertainment media."

☆ ☆

Scores of celebrities have since been a part of Leo's culinary adventures, and clients such as the California Turkey Advisory Board, the California Potato Board, Frito-Lay and Mrs. Cubbison's Dressing Mix (a 50-year-long client!) have feasted on the resulting national publicity. In fact, Leo holds the distinction of having known the original Mrs. Cubbison herself.

Today, two of Leo and Helen's sons, Howard and Frank, are both principals of the agency. Howard, who has a degree in public relations, has been in the profession for over 30 years and Frank, who has a degree in journalism, for over 20 years. They also contributed their valuable experience to this book. The oldest of their three sons, David, is a successful music composer and music producer who has also worked on music projects for agency clients. Lee & Associates is truly a "home grown" family business, having started three generations ago in a mom-and-pop grocery market.

Look what Jack Webb caught in his "Dragnet."

Bing carves a turkey on his popular TV show.

More importantly, we hope to impart to you just how to create those successes. This book will take you "behind the scenes" to share with you how many of these accomplishments developed. You will be entertained as much as you will be informed. The general philosophy and operation that developed early in the business continues on through today. It is the type of education that you learn only in the "school of hard knocks." While this book addresses classic public relations situations, it also offers appealing advice to any person who must use tact and diplomacy in the everyday "public relations" of life.

This book represents years of publicity at its best and its funniest! It is a collection of anecdotes and classic celebrity photos that tell the agency's story over a half-century. It highlights many special experiences that have befallen Lee & Associates as the company grew. While Leo has completed his next book: "*Recipes Of The Stars*," he shares some of his favorite recipes in this book, as well. Chapter 22 includes recipes from the likes of Bob Hope, Mickey Rooney, Bill Cosby, and Phyllis Diller. So, come join Leo and his family in reliving many of their funniest, and most rewarding, growing pains in the world of public relations.

The Pearlstein family photographed at a black-tie event. (l. to r.) Leo, Helen, David, Howard and Frank.

Introduction: Food For Thought

☆ ☆

Everyone likes to eat, and almost everyone trusts what celebrities and other public figures tell us to eat. I made a career out of combining food with recognizable faces. I put nutritious foods together with well-known personalities to assist in promoting movies, television shows, charitable causes and fun festivities, from conservative to zany. Additionally, I provide national food editors and columnists with feature stories and photos, working with such influential people as home economists, doctors, teachers, chefs, and dieticians. As a public relations (PR) counselor representing various food industries and products, I often called upon prominent people in my publicity endeavors, which led to my being closely involved with the entertainment industry. I learned that celebrities are able to reach the largest audiences. Over the years, I have presented the entertainment media with a variety of products for news features and for background exposure in movies and television, providing everything from chives to turkeys.

I got into this business by planting a few seeds—almost literally. I like dealing with people and communicating with them. Informing and educating people has always appealed to me, and the best way to do that is by entertaining the audience. Then, when you get someone's attention, you can slip in a little information. Food is a popular item; everyone has to eat, but it can get boring like anything else. It occurred to me that I could tell people what to do with it, create new recipes for them, show them better and quicker ways to serve foods, and introduce them to healthy products they may not have known how to prepare. My strategy was to get entertainers and other celebrities to pose with the food products, then promotionally, everyone would benefit: the film studios, my food industry clientele, and the general public. These few seedling ideas were sown into fertile soil that has generated a ton of positive, national publicity over the decades. My Los Angeles-based public relations and advertising agency, Lee & Associates, Inc., has maintained ongoing, longterm relationships with our clients and members of the entertainment industry for a half century—highly unusual in today's PR business. I have been fortunate to work with many talent agents and managers who helped set up the photo sessions with their celebrities for me. My 50 years in the PR and publicity business has yielded a bumper crop of friends, colleagues, and healthy, hearty (and well-informed) audiences!

At the dawn of this exciting new millennium, I am celebrating the

☆ ☆

golden anniversary of my adventures in publicity. I've worked with the Hollywood television and motion picture industries, from supplying food products for television talk-show segments and celebrity charity events, to celebrity photo sessions and even for movie props. Ever wonder where all the groceries come from when you see a movie with a super- market setting? Chances are that I, or one of my public relations col- leagues, hauled many of them over to the soundstages in our station wagons.

I am proud to be one of the earliest members of the Academy of Tele- vision Arts & Sciences. I still remain active and also vote each year for the shows I feel should receive an Emmy Award. My membership in the TV Academy proved invaluable in helping me connect with TV stars.

I would like to take you on a nostalgic tour of that Hollywood of yesterday and share with you some of our many "fruitful" adventures. They were often hilarious, outrageous, surprising—and almost always fun, fun, fun!

Celebrities posed with my clients' products for a variety of reasons which were beneficial to them and the studios: 1) They may have had a movie or TV show to promote and we could provide them with publicity outside the typical Hollywood media; 2) A specific tie-in existed between what they were promoting and what we were promoting; 3) Since I often represented generic products, I was able to assist newspapers with setting up photo sessions; 4) I often donated food to be served at vari- ous charity and special-event functions which were attended by celebri- ties, and they were happy to pose with the volunteers serving the food products, which resulted in additional publicity; 5) I was able to create awards to garner publicity that were mutually beneficial to my clients and the celebrities; 6) I was able to provide a public service venue to talk about the basic food groups and nutrition via radio announcements.

I have had the pleasure of working with such Hollywood royalty as Steve Allen, Abbott & Costello, Jack Lemmon, Sammy Davis Jr., Doris Day, Bob Hope, Jayne Mansfield, Dinah Shore, Bob Cummings, Dennis Weaver, Walt Disney's original Mouseketeers, Groucho Marx, James Mason, Fred MacMurray, Perry Como, Mickey Rooney, Andy Griffith, Bill Cosby, Art Linkletter, Tennessee Ernie Ford, Jimmy Durante, Bob Barker, Wayne Newton, Eddie Bracken (my original boss), Diahann Car- roll, and Jerry Lewis, among many others. Some notables have included U.S. Presidents John Kennedy and Gerald Ford, California Governors Goodwin Knight, Edmund (Pat) Brown, Jerry Brown and Ronald Reagan.

☆ ☆

I also enjoyed working with Senators Alan Cranston of California and Everett Dirkson of Illinois, San Diego Mayor Pete Wilson, who later became a California governor, and Los Angeles Mayors Norris Poulson, Sam Yorty, Tom Bradley and Richard Riordan. Also, there were well-known sports figures such as baseball's Dave Winfield, football's Rosie Grier, and Joe Theisman, boxing champions Mohammed Ali and George Foreman, and Olympic gold medalist Mark Spitz. What a great mixture of special people—I call it my "Celebrity Stew."

In television's early days in the 1950s and '60s, many of the shows were presented "live," as opposed to being pre-recorded on videotape. A simple segment about the promotion of a food product—for example, prunes—could stretch into an uproarious comedy routine in the hands of skilled artists such as Steve Allen or Dinah Shore. Not only were audiences told about the many healthy virtues of prunes and different ways to serve them, but they were entertained, as if the segment had nothing to do with promoting a product.

The teacher in me would like to show you how it was all done: to go beyond the "smoke and mirrors," which is a term often used to describe publicity activities. There really are no smoke and mirrors. There really is no magic. I will take you onto the backlots of Hollywood and other places to demonstrate how the right combination of creativity, hard work, cooperation, and goodwill can start a chain reaction of abundant publicity that didn't cost anyone megabucks. While it is my hope you will be informed and entertained with this book, I also wish to impart the highest *value and meaning* of "Public Relations" (a.k.a. PR) as it can be applied to any campaign promoting a person, product, service, place, or thing. Ethics and standards apply, as well as boundaries that must be mutually respected. It is a matter of using your creativity and doing the work. For those of you who are students of public relations, I hope to pass along information and inspiration that you will never learn in the classroom, so that you can reach out for your greatest dreams.

Hollywood has changed in the 50 years that I have been privileged to be a part of its exciting and attractive society. At the end of the book, I will compare the "then and now" of how Hollywood operates, and how the changes have affected the obtaining of positive publicity. Unlike many other corporate arenas, the film capital accepts the importance of public relations and the value of publicity; movies could not succeed without it. Outside the film industry, some of the highest qualified executives in the world don't know what public relations really is all about, or how it works. Public relations, publicity, merchandising and advertising all work together in the promotion and sale of anything or anyone, especially if the product or service being marketed is to be a success.

It is better to have an influential person tell people about your product. People, such as a newspaper food editor, or a TV or radio personality, can reach the masses and are trusted and believed. As you will see, further along in the book, if a celebrity genuinely likes a product, the publicity will spawn itself naturally after a certain point. That is when the magic factor called "word of mouth" catches on, and all the efforts to inform and educate really work! The client is happy; the celebrity, movie or TV show has additional exposure; and the public has been introduced to something it likes and did not know was available.

We, at Lee & Associates, Inc., hope you will enjoy these stories presented in the book and, like we did, learn from the mistakes and the unexpected everyday occurrences—the emergencies, the opportunities and the successes—which are all a part of life. It is a great feeling when things come together. It always gave us, and still gives us, great pleasure as the reward for our work. At the same time, we have learned to roll with the punches when things go wrong and make them right again. This is a glamorous business with lots of excitement. It is very stimulating, but there is plenty of "grunt" work along the way.

What is Public Relations?

Over the years, when I have given lectures and appeared on TV and radio interviews, I have been asked to define PR. Before you take the plunge into this book, I would like to offer my favorite definitions and anecdotes on the subject, which offer a humorous, but very revealing, insight into how this business works. There are many textbook definitions of PR that I like. Most professionals describe PR as a "direct effort to influence the attitudes and opinions of people in a favorable way." The dictionary definition calls PR "the business of fostering public goodwill toward a person, firm, or institution, and the degree of goodwill and understanding achieved." Another favorite of mine comes out of a PR textbook titled Communication and Public Relations by Edward Robinson. It states: "Public relations is the management function which evaluates public attitudes, identifies the policies and procedures of an individual or an organization with the public interest, and plans and executes a program of action to earn public understanding and acceptance."

Several years ago, I saw a cute story about the definition of public relations; it goes like this:

☆ ☆

A Norwegian man, who was visiting Madison Avenue in New York, asked an executive at an advertising agency what public relations was all about; he had never heard of such a business in Norway. (We were later to learn that the Japanese language has no definition for "public relations," either.) The advertising man replied as follows: "When you are taking out a young lady, and you want to impress her, you tell her how good you are, how much money you make, what a great catch you would be, and really brag about yourself—that is advertising! Then, when you start bringing her flowers and candy, and take her to the best plays and events—that is merchandising. But when you arrange for her best friend or someone she trusts to tell her how good you are—that is public relations! PR is a language spoken in the 'third person.' It takes a third person, an outside party, to talk-up the merits of a product, an idea, another person—or anything."

There is another definition of PR that I have often thought of engraving on a plaque and hanging on my wall. One of our friends said that "Advertising is paying, and public relations is praying." In other words, in advertising, you pay for the space where your ad will appear. However, in public relations, we pray that our news stories get used by the media, as we are at their mercy and news judgment. Sometimes, even with the best of intentions on the part of a newspaper, radio, or TV station, good publicity generated by a PR person may bite the dust in favor of the coverage of another more timely story, or even a catastrophic event, such as only mother nature can provide. I've included just such a chapter in the book. It describes incredible, almost unbelievable, foul luck in having terrific national publicity stories booted off the front pages because of untimely, devastating "acts of God" or perversions of man and fate.

Mostly, public relations stories are success stories, like my favorite, that of Paul Revere. Everyone learns about Revolutionary War hero Paul Revere in school; he was immortalized in Henry Wadsworth Longfellow's poem, "Paul Revere's Ride." His name even reappeared as the name of a popular rock group a couple centuries later in the 1960's, Paul Revere and the Raiders. What we didn't learn in school is that two other people—William Dawes and Samuel Prescott—were with him on that harrowing trip to Concord in 1775, when Revere set out to warn people along the way that "the British are coming!" Dawes and Prescott were just as much involved in the midnight mission as Revere. In fact, Revere was actually detained by British scouts en route, and only Prescott made

☆ ☆

it all the way to Concord where he warned the townsfolk of the impending arrival of the British. Why do we remember Paul Revere? Well, he was a true public relations man. Everybody knew Paul Revere because he was involved in all the community activities. He was a local businessman, a silversmith, and he promoted himself wherever possible. He was an activist. He was involved. He was all over the place. And people knew him, so it seems natural that the poet Longfellow would pick someone who was already known. In my estimation, Paul Revere could be considered the first public relations person.

As you travel through this book, you will notice how communications has changed in the last half-century of the past millennium. But certain basic PR principles remain forever. These are the ones we follow:

1. A public relations formula we use with the acronym R.A.C.E. (Research, Analysis, Communication and Evaluation)
2. Offer the media timely, contemporary suggestions
3. Offer the media accurate, well-researched facts
4. Provide good information that newspaper and magazine editors will want to share with their readers
5. Offer good programming for radio and television. The public relations consultant has an obligation to not only inform, but to entertain and to educate the radio or TV audience, as well, using serious and/or humorous material. You cannot just go on the air and get a free plug. There has to be a purpose.

It seems the faster we grow and evolve, the more we are headed "back" to those primary elements that give us grounding. That is why nostalgia appeals to our senses. We can laugh at the antics of yesteryear, but the creativity and spontaneity of those early television days seem to intrigue us. We still wonder how it was all done, like unraveling the mystery of the Great Pyramids in Egypt. What still keeps the world of commerce turning is the barter-and-trade and helping out your fellow humans, both socially and in business.

We have more and better opportunities to interact with each other today. To me, that is an exciting thing to look forward to in this new millennium. Can you imagine how well known Paul Revere would have been with cable television or the Internet at his disposal? If I had lived in his time, I would certainly have wanted him to use and be seen with my clients' products! He would have been a superstar.

I trust that I have given you much food for thought before I show

☆ ☆

you how Hollywood and I, and the many fine people with whom I have worked in this business, sought to promote a healthier American public through some pretty zany media exposure.

Mr. Pearlstein goes to Washington— to address a high-level conference on "How to Reach the Disadvantaged with Nutrition Information."

When TV Guide wanted to know about product placement in TV and movies, they went to the sources, one of which was Leo Pearlstein. This major feature article was published June 17, 1978.

1

Jayne Mansfield and the Great Turkey Barter

☆ ☆

I remember how much I enjoyed working with Jayne Mansfield. She was smart, very nice, friendly and extremely professional. She was also very devoted to her children and to her family who lived in Dallas, Texas.

Jayne became famous in the 1950s for her exaggerated sexy appearance and her many publicity stunts. In 1957, she was starring in a Twentieth Century Fox movie called "Will Success Spoil Rock Hunter?" It occurred to me that Jayne had recently been on hand to cut the ribbon at various supermarket openings and thus, received ongoing publicity. Supermarket openings were a good way for up-and-coming stars to get a lot of public exposure in those days.

At that time, we were looking for an attention-getting event to motivate supermarkets to feature turkey, on behalf of our client, the California Turkey Advisory Board. To impress the supermarket retailers, we were looking for a promotional idea that would really shake them up. We called the publicity director at Twentieth Century Fox and told him we would like to do a tie-in and get publicity for both Jayne and the turkey industry. We had a new apron we created with "How About a TURKEY Bar B-Q" printed on

Jayne posing in our Bar B-Q apron.

Jayne presents the finished turkey.

it. We wanted someone to wear that apron who could call a great deal of attention to it, thus drawing attention to the turkey industry. Jayne could add some glamor to our promotion, getting us more media exposure.

The Twentieth Century Fox executives cooperated and said it was a great idea, but we would have to contact her manager/agent. That's when we ran into a bottleneck, because he was one tough guy! "Jayne just got paid $3,500 for cutting a ribbon at the Better Foods Market," he told me. That was a whopping big sum in 1957, and it made my eyeballs spin.

"That's great," I said, "but we are not paying—we're publicizing—and if she works with us, we will triple her publicity."

Much discussion ensued and he wouldn't give in, so we decided to barter with him using turkeys. We ended up agreeing to give her 26 turkeys and send four more to her parents in Texas, if we could do a photo session at her house promoting turkeys. We met with Jayne at her home; she liked the idea of the photo shoot and told us to work with her housekeeper regarding the turkey exchange. Whenever her housekeeper wanted to cook a turkey, she would call us and we would set up a delivery. Naturally, we wanted to deliver the bird ourselves instead of having the local turkey processor deliver it. After all, it was Hollywood—show biz!—and quite exciting to be dealing with Jayne Mansfield. Every time we delivered a turkey we would credit the account in her name.

After we made these arrangements, we set up a photo session and had one of Hollywood's top photographers, Bob Perkins, who did photo stills of many movie stars, come out to her house with all of his equipment. We cooked up a huge turkey to put on her barbecue. When Jayne appeared, I explained our promotional concept to her, about how turkey is great to eat anytime, not just on special holiday occasions. I also told her one of the best ways to cook turkey is on a barbecue. She donned our apron, and looked like a very glamorous cook. We shot several photos of her while she tended to the barbecued turkey. Jayne also changed into something diffferent for the photos, an attractive all-cotton, white halter top outfit. Not only did she look like a stunning movie beauty, the turkey never looked finer either, as Jayne posed to carve it. We shot quite a variety of photos to use for media news releases.

We developed the pictures and sent them out to all the Hollywood media, as well as to media around the country, with a caption reading "Jayne Mansfield loves to barbecue turkey." We would also give added publicity to her latest film at Twentieth Century Fox. We got great media coverage. Jayne was happy, the studio was happy, and our client was happy.

Our BIG success came when we sent this photo out to all the major supermarket meat buyers in the area. Practically everyone pinned up the Jayne Mansfield photo in his buying office, and every gro-

Seasoning the turkey.

Healthy eating promotes a healthy body.

cery and meat trade publication used the photo for publicity. It is not every day you see a photo of a glamorous movie star in a trade publication, which is outside the mainstream media of newspapers and magazines; but that wasn't the end of it. We kept delivering turkeys to Jayne over the next several months, and we were down to our last turkey when she announced that she was going to marry famous muscleman Mickey Hargitay, a former Mr. Universe. We sent a turkey out to Jayne the day before the wedding with a note saying, "Congratulations! Happy Wedding! Enjoy the Turkey!" The wedding was covered by a multitude of photographers, including a crew from Life magazine. The Life magazine reporter who attended asked Jayne, "Now that you are married, what are you going to do about cooking?"

Jayne replied in her giggly, purring voice, "I love turkey! It tastes so good, especially barbecued! I'll be cooking them often, not just for the holidays. Anytime is turkey time."

Life magazine was as popular in the 1950s as People magazine is today, so you can imagine how happy and fortunate we were to get this plug for turkeys in one of the most popular national magazines. Maybe it was a lucky break for us that her manager/agent had originally been so stubborn a negotiator, because all that turkey bartering really paid off!

We even got Jayne's young daughter into the act.

Leo promoting that "Anytime Is Turkey Time"—especially with Jayne Mansfield.

2

"Anytime Is Turkey Time"

☆ ☆

The Jayne Mansfield adventure lead to a promotion that lasted almost 20 years. Even though the word "turkey" in show business denotes a "flop," celebrities were most cooperative in helping us remind the public that "anytime is turkey time," a theme I developed in the '50s to promote the turkey industry the year 'round. The term "turkey" as a flop spread as a result of an experience on Broadway. When new shows opened on New York's Broadway in the early days on Thanksgiving Day, they hardly had any audiences. It became apparent that this day was meant for the family to get together at home, and not for going to the theater. So, the shows were a "flop" and thus, the connection with being a "turkey."

We had a good story to tell. In the 1950s, California was the largest producer of turkeys. Turkey was recognized as certainly being tasty and healthy, too, being high in protein and low in fat. To promote our client, the California Turkey Advisory Board, we contacted many people in the entertainment industry and suggested that we would be happy to help promote their movie, TV show, or theatrical projects. We would have fun and use photo captions with celebrities "talking turkey." In many cases, we added their favorite turkey recipes. To thank them, we were very liberal with distributing turkeys to the stars, especially at Thanksgiving.

Over the years, we often worked as a team with the Turkey Board's hardworking manager, Gene Beals, who helped with the planning and participated in many of the special events.

Following are some of my favorite celebrities, photographed during the promotion of turkeys during the '50s and '60s.

☆ ☆ ☆ ☆ ☆ ☆ ☆ ☆ ☆ ☆ ☆ ☆ ☆ ☆ ☆ ☆ ☆ ☆ ☆ ☆

Ozzie and Harriet Nelson

Shirley McLaine

Stan Freberg

James and Pamela Mason

Buddy Hackett

Jeanne Carmen

Jo Stafford

Art Baker

Julie London, Bobby Troupe

☆☆☆☆☆☆☆☆☆☆☆☆☆☆☆☆☆☆☆☆☆

Calif. Gov. Goodwin Knight

Gracie Allen

Ray Anthony, Mamie Van Doran

Jack Carson, Lola Albright

Irish "Sheena" McCalla

George Gobel

Bob Cummings, Rosemary De Camp

"Queen for a Day"

Emcee, Jack Bailey

3

Abbott & Costello Lay A Golden Egg

☆ ☆

Abbott & Costello was one of the greatest comedy teams in the history of show business. Their particular blend of straight-man and funny sidekick brought success to them in five entertainment media: the vaudeville stage, radio, Broadway, movies, and television. While appearing on the "Kate Smith Radio Hour" in the late 1930s, they debuted their classic signature skit, "Who's On First?," one that would hurl them to fame, fortune and Hollywood. To this day, "Who's On First?" remains one of the funniest comedy routines on record.

The 1940s brought them one box-office hit after another, including the international cult classic "Abbott & Costello Meet Frankenstein." Their tremendous success carried over easily into the new medium of television in the early 1950s. They were one of the early pioneers of episodic television, with a two-season run of the popular "Abbott & Costello Show" (1951-'52). Their clean style of comedy has withstood the difficult "test of time" and still captivates audiences in the ever-competitive entertainment marketplace.

Bud Abbott and Lou Costello help promote eggs.

My association with Bud Abbott and Lou Costello came at the height of their fame in 1952. It all began when I read in Daily Variety that the famous funny duo was filming their movie version of "Jack and the Beanstalk." Just imagining Abbott & Costello in the children's classic story could incite laughter before the film was even released. It was guaranteed to be a success. Of course, the story highlights the proverbial "golden egg" of fairy-tale fable: another tie-in advantage for us.

As we represented the Pacific Dairy and Poultry Association at the time, it was our job to promote eggs. What better way to draw attention to them than to use these two famous comedians, their movie, and the golden egg. We just knew we could come up with an eye-catching way to promote the golden-egg theme, so you might say we "scrambled" to get our client in the limelight with the movie. For starters, we contacted the publicity department at Warner Brothers Studios, proposing that if they would help us, we would help publicize the movie in return. After going through many channels, we ended up with Abbott & Costello's personal publicity agent, telling him we would like to work with the popular comedy team and play up the golden-egg idea. It was a natural tie-in. We had access to millions of cartons of eggs. We could promote the movie by putting a promotional announcement in the egg cartons and, at the same time, encourage people to eat more eggs.

Another big idea began to simmer in our pot. The Pacific Dairy and Poultry

Egg carton insert—we sold eggs by the dozen, they sold movie tickets by the million.

Association had scheduled a major convention in the historic Hotel Del Coronado near San Diego, California. Known locally as the Hotel Del, the sprawling resort—noted for its unique architecture—was built in 1888 and has accommodated many U.S. presidents and public figures. It is even reputed to be the place where England's King Edward VIII first met Wallis Warfield Simpson, for whom he would ultimately give up the throne to marry. Given the palatial hotel's exciting history, we thought it would be a great idea to have Abbott & Costello add to it by showing up at the dairy and poultry convention. In fact, it was rather gutsy of us to even encourage the thought of getting this highly sought-after comedy team to appear on our program schedule. But the famed comedy team was so impressed that we were going to do lots of publicity, apart from the normal "Hollywood" type of PR, that they actually agreed. Barring an act of God, Abbott & Costello would drive 150 miles down to the Hotel Del Coronado and be guests at our "Big Egg Breakfast." They would be among other distinguished company: the U.S. Secretary of Agriculture, Charles F. Brannan, a Democrat, and Governor J. Bracken Lee of Utah, a Republican, were the guests of honor. Here we had both political parties represented, and we were going to sit down and eat eggs together.

We then hatched our golden plan. We would serve up a giant egg breakfast, with the theme "Two Eggs For You in '52." Believe it or not, we located a huge frying pan that was 10 feet in diameter. A Holly-

The incomparable Del Coronado Hotel near San Diego, California.

wood prop man who worked at one of the major studios knew how to get hold of such things; he was accustomed to unusual requests. He told us where we could find a gargantuan skillet. We borrowed it from the Chamber of Commerce of a small town in Washington, which loaned it to us for the goodwill and fun of it all, as well as for any publicity that would benefit them. We made arrangements for the chamber to ship the frying pan down to us in Los Angeles, which was no easy feat in itself. From there, we would send it on to the Hotel Del Coronado. Transporting a giant frying pan caused as many headaches as if we had been hit over the head with it. The pan was so big, it wouldn't fit in a standard truck. It had to be hauled on a special flatbed truck. We also arranged to take the frying pan to Warner Brothers studios so we could take a picture of Abbott & Costello with our executives getting ready for the big event. Only in Hollywood, the film capital of the world, does a 10-foot frying pan riding down the street on a flatbed truck not look particularly conspicuous. If this were any other city, people would have thought we were nuts.

Prior to the giant egg breakfast, we sent out the usual publicity releases to the media. Then something extraordinary happened which gave us an unexpected promotional bonus. A farmer in Utah, who had seen one of our stories in a trade paper, called us and said he owned a chicken that had literally laid a golden egg. Come on now! But, astonish-

Special 10-foot frying pan helped draw extra attention to our egg promotion.

ing as it was, the egg turned out to be real! We had it insured and flown to Los Angeles. We made a big fuss about the event and took pictures of it arriving by plane. The precious egg had been washed, sanded, scraped, candled and otherwise inspected by several poultry experts from the University of California at Riverside. They proved it was a real egg, not a phony. But how could that be? The experts thought that possibly the chicken had been sick and had produced a colored egg due to illness. Or maybe the chicken's feed had produced the odd-colored egg, which was worth a lot more to us than "chicken feed," let me tell you! Whatever the cause, this one egg was the only golden-yellow specimen the chicken had yielded. Perhaps it truly was the fairy-tale Golden Egg!

The first thing we did was to insure the egg with Lloyds of London for a million dollars, which was purely a promotional gimmick. Then we took photos of Abbott & Costello at the studios with the golden egg and the Lloyds of London insurance policy. As a result of those priceless photos, we got a tremendous amount of exposure, especially in the egg industry and retail market publications. To give you a real good idea of the impact of this publicity, the Utah farmer thought that his egg was actually worth a fortune. He got in touch with us again, this time wanting us to pay him a large amount of money. I think he asked for about $10,000. Well, we turned around, put the egg in a box very carefully, packed it, shipped it back by plane and thanked him very much for use of the egg.

The second phase of our public relations plan was to promote Abbott & Costello coming to Coronado for the big convention. Of course, we told the entire egg and poultry industry that they were coming. That was pretty heady stuff for two such major headliners as Abbott & Costello to be guests of honor, plus Secretary of Agriculture Brannan and Governor Lee of Utah, who had traveled to California especially for the convention. We shipped our big frying pan down to the Hotel Del Coronado and planned our giant breakfast. But the night before the convention was to open, a terrific rainstorm pelted the Southern California area, an unusual occurrence because, like the song says, "it never rains in Southern California" (except when you're planning a major PR event). We got a phone call from Abbott & Costello's agent saying, "Sorry, but they can't come to the convention; we can't afford to lose any extra time. We have to finish shooting the movie." The "Jack and the Beanstalk" producers also couldn't take a chance on the comedy team getting sick by being out in the stormy weather.

So, here we were with all of our promises, and the next day I

☆ ☆

had to tell the association leaders that our "stars" were not coming. Some of the leaders understood, but many did not. We never before realized how movie-struck people can be. We soon became the convention-eers' scapegoats. Many were disappointed and mad. What should we do? I had to get up in front of 1,000 conventioneers and inform them that, due to circumstances beyond our control, mainly the big storm, Abbott & Costello would not be able to come.

In the meantime, we thought, "What should we do about the media?" I was sure that most of them understand that these things can happen. But we had movie publicists, TV news crews, wire services and newspaper reporters showing up; they were our captive audience! At least we still had the giant frying pan. We decided to take that big skillet and cook up 1,000 eggs right there in the conven-

Utah Governor Lee (l.) and U.S. Secretary of Agriculture Brannan flip eggs for the TV and newspaper cameras.

tion room. We would have the Secretary of Agriculture and the Governor of Utah flipping eggs and saying kind words about nutrition. But the fire marshal told us, "No fires in the Hotel Del Coronado." The "grand dame" of hotels was made of very old wood. In fact, it's one of the largest all-wood structures in the world. There-fore, it had water sprinklers sticking out everywhere. Without a doubt, the sprinklers

Cooked eggs were served from the giant frying pan.

would turn on and ruin our big breakfast event photos.

What could we do now? We went into the kitchen, made a deal with the chef, and he cooked up the fried eggs for us under the fire law safety of his turf. When they were ready, we took them back to the convention room and put them into the frying pan so we could have our photo session. Everything worked out okay. We had a few unhappy conventioneers and industry leaders who had wanted to see Abbott & Costello. But, we obtained a lot of good, positive publicity for the Pacific Dairy and Poultry Association, and they got an excellent egg breakfast.

Lou gets the girl (Ginger Crawley)—Bud gets the insurance policy.

4

"Good Eggs" and Golden Egg Awards

☆ ☆

Our Golden Egg adventures resulted in a long period of celebrity connections, on behalf of our client, the California Egg Commission. We purchased gold-plated eggs and created little wooden stands to hold them. This made an interesting display, and thus we created the Golden Egg Award. We sought out celebrities directly or through their publicity agents. We served eggs (mostly hard-cooked) at many high-visibility events, such as the "Jerry Lewis Telethon," "Celebrity Tennis," "Celebrity Bowling" and many charity events. We asked the celebrities if they wouldn't mind posing with our volunteer spokespersons and we would present them with a Golden Egg Award for being a "good egg" for their participation in the charity event. It was fun and it certainly drew attention to the celebrities, the charity, and of course, eggs. We offered to help with publicity and relate the Golden Egg awards to their own activities. This also gave us an opportunity to mention the nutritional benefits of eggs. Following are some of my favorite celebrities photographed during the promotion of eggs from the '50s through the '70s.

Regis Philbin (r.) discussing egg white facial benefits with dermatologist, Dr. Jerome Litt on KHJ-TV, Los Angeles.

Cesar Romero

Frank Sinatra, Jr.

Chad Everett, Karen Lindsey

Bozo, young Frankie Pearlstein

Dinah Shore, Norm Crosby, square eggs

Joseph Campanella, Karen Lindsey

☆ ☆

Dr. L.A. Wilhelm, Art Linkletter

Doc Severinson, Karen Lindsey, Ed McMahon

Richard Harris

Valerie Perrine

"Skipper Frank" Hermann

Karen Lindsey, Wayne Rodgers

Kid TV's "Sheriff John" Rovick

5

Promoting Potatoes — From Groucho to Mickey Mouse

☆ ☆

Groucho and the Potato Salad Deluge

It's funny the way things come together in life. I have been asked many times how I got the legendary Groucho Marx—whose trademark was cigars—to pose with potatoes. Somehow, one just did not associate the wiry-thin comedian with food. If you've seen his hilarious movies from the 1930s and his TV show in reruns, you know how his suits always appeared to hang on him, as if he were underfed. He, of all people, needed a few potatoes in his diet.

Groucho enjoying homemade potato salad, delivered by an admiring fan.

Groucho Marx' television game show, "You Bet Your Life," was a popular quiz program with an early talk-show format in the 1950s. The show was a strong hit during television's Golden Age. During each segment, two guests came on stage and Groucho would draw them out with his dry wit, asking them ridiculous—often embarrassing—questions about themselves or their line of work, before giving them a chance to acquire a few hundred dollars in a quiz. His guests certainly earned it! Groucho's quick, subtle humor was unrelenting. Everything was fair game for his barbs. When we took on the California Potato Advisory Board as a client, little did

☆ ☆ ☆ ☆ ☆ ☆ ☆ ☆ ☆ ☆ ☆ ☆ ☆ ☆ ☆ ☆ ☆ ☆ ☆ ☆

we dream we had a product ripe for Groucho's humorous pickings.

The potato board was headquartered in Bakersfield, in central California, where a great deal of the state's produce is grown. The California Long White potato, which we were hired to promote, is a specific hybrid that's literally longer and whiter in color than the common Russet potato. It is part of the White Rose family, very thin-skinned, and the first potatoes of the season.

We did all the promotional basics, working with newspaper and magazine food editors, radio and TV shows, cooking schools, dietitians, home economists, and so on. In the publicity we generated, we pointed out that the bulk of calories are not "in" the potatoes, but are in what you put "on" them. We had plenty of good, educational material with which to work. We created many marketing tie-ins, even to the point of getting a record company to record a song about potatoes. You name it, we did it, but the potato farmers never seemed to be happy. They were always looking for something "more exciting." That is the expectation of a lot of clients. As I mentioned, there are certain basic things you have to do to market any product. That exciting "something more"—like sports figures, celebrities, movie stars, or crazy stunts—revs a client up when they get exposure of their product.

All of which brings me back to Groucho. It just so happened that his offices were in the building next to ours. This was not only convenient but, also a lucky break for me and certainly the potato industry. His close proximity enabled us to eliminate many of the usual channels in reaching the immensely popular comedian. We pondered on how to get potatoes on his show. One of the potato board directors, who was also a leading potato grower, lived in nearby Riverside, only an hour's drive from Los Angeles. He could easily drive in for the show, and fortunately, potatoes are a tasty subject for conversation. There's so much you can do with potatoes: fry them, boil them, mash them, bake them. Surely it would be easy to get Groucho involved in a funny conversation with our client and get plenty of plugs for the California Long White potato. Not to detract from the potato, but it seemed like "a piece of cake," a very easy job.

Knowing Groucho's penchant for offbeat jokes, we recommended our potato grower as an excellent potential guest for Groucho's "You Bet Your Life" which, remember, was one of the hottest shows of early television. The potato grower was interviewed and quickly accepted by the production staff. To keep his humor fresh and spontaneous, Groucho never even saw his guests until he met them when they first walked out onstage. He would be given a 3"x 5" card with only essential information about each contestant and from that, he would ask the questions.

We coached the potato grower to be prepared for Groucho's unusual questions and told him that, regardless of what went on, he should get in a good plug for "California Long White potatoes." As a rule, Groucho would start out the conversation with something innocuous like "And what do you do, sir?" We told our potato grower to say, "I grow California Long White potatoes, the best potatoes in the land." Our client was quite enthusiastic and was very well prepared to plug his product. In those days, Groucho's show was live, so it was possible to say just about anything on the air, as long as Groucho would allow it.

Just before the show's date, we literally contacted everyone in the nation's potato industry, telling them to be sure to watch "You Bet Your Life" and see our promotion for California Long White potatoes. On the evening the show aired, I sat in the studio audience with the chairman and the manager of the potato advisory board—two very politically important members—and watched as our guest, John McSweeny, went on national television to plug potatoes. This was quite a coup for us because, in the early 1950s, television was still a new medium, barely up and toddling. We didn't have the multitude of shows, not to mention the many channels and networks, that abound today.

Right off the bat, we got a surprise. Instead of the usual question, "What do you do?," Groucho veered off on a tangent and asked where John had gone to college and what had been his college major, which turned out to be engineering, a subject completely unrelated to the potato story we had John rehearse. So, Groucho led John off on a conversation about what engineers do. He asked John every conceivable question about engineering, none of which was even remotely related to the California Long White potato. In fact, it would have taken a quantum leap to get from engineering to potatoes. Some of you may be familiar with a Hollywood trivia game that, like charades, currently travels around party circles. One person names a movie and its star, and the object is to relate the star to another movie—and another, and another—until way down the line the star is linked with another star or movie that can be traced, step by step, back to the original movie named at the beginning of the game. Whew! As you can imagine, that's how I felt waiting for Groucho to get, step by step, to the important subject—potatoes! I kept wondering when the plug would come. Would it be after the next ques-

tion, or the next, or would we reach the end of the show without connecting the dots to the California Long White potato? I began to worry, if not pray. My sure thing was suddenly something I wouldn't bet *my* life on!

Cringing as I sat in the audience, I was bracing myself for the potato growers to accuse me of wasting their time on this, because Groucho was about to start the game and there was no plug yet for the California Long White potato. "Oh pleeeze, just say anything that will lead to mention of the potato," I thought to myself, as I sweated out the remaining minutes of the show. "I'll take any plug. I'm desperate. Even the 'secret word!'" As Groucho aficionados know, if any guest said the "secret word" during the show, a toy duck would fly down from the rafters bearing a card in its mouth with the word on it. Band music played, and the show was temporarily halted. The guest who unwittingly said the "secret word" would be rewarded with a $50 or $100 bill. "Oh, please let the secret word be 'potato' tonight, pleeeeeezzzze!" I brightened. Maybe that's what the producers of the show had planned!

Just as they were running out of time for John's interview, Groucho nonchalantly asked him, "So what do you do?" At last, the standard question we had all been waiting for! Trouper that he was, John proudly proclaimed, "I grow California Long White potatoes, the best potatoes in the land!"

Then we got an unexpected bonus. Before John had a chance to say anything else, Groucho said, "Do you have a good potato salad recipe? I like German potato salad." Oh what luck! Groucho liked potatoes!

"I don't have it with me," John replied, "but I will be glad to get you plenty of recipes." Boom! We got our plug! Mission accomplished, even if it was through the back door.

Believe it or not, to our surprise, the next day we saw endless cars —including limousines and taxicabs—driving up to Groucho's office, delivering bowls and containers of potato salad that had been made by many of Groucho's loyal viewers. Remember, it was the very early days of television when we were all in awe of the new medium's power to reach the public. Just the bare mention that Groucho liked potato salad had brought every conceivable recipe to his door. To show our own appreciation, we delivered potatoes to all of Groucho's employees.

Then the mail came! For about five days, bags and bags of mail poured into Groucho's office. There must have been well over 5,000 potato salad recipes. We went over and took a photo of Groucho with potato salad and some of the thousands of recipes piled high on his desk.

☆ ☆

Unfortunately, a few days later when we asked for all those thousands of recipes, we learned they had been thrown out by an obviously unsentimental, and unthinking, employee. How I wish I had them today; they would make a whole book in themselves.

Here is a very important rule that comes to mind. Never assume anything. Those are good words to the wise, both in business and in life. We just "assumed" that Groucho's office was going to turn over all those wonderful potato recipes to us, since they knew we were working for the potato industry and they must have known it meant a lot to us. From then on, whenever we trained a new staff member, we pointed to a notice on our bulletin board that read, **"NEVER ASSUME."**

A spoon-fed Groucho amidst his mountain of potato salad recipes.

☆ ☆

Andy Griffith Gets the Potato Bug in His Ear

Another adventure in my on-going potato saga occurred when I visited with an old friend back east, Dick Link, who was Andy Griffith's personal manager in the early '50s. Dick introduced me to Andy who occasionally appeared on the "Perry Como Show." This was many years prior to the immensely popular "Andy Griffith Show," which made Andy an American television icon and also launched the multi-faceted career of child star Ron Howard who is now a famous film director. When I knew him, Andy was just becoming well known in the business and had made a couple of hit comedy records that were essentially recorded monologues. The drawling Southern comedian was constantly looking for new ideas, so I suggested his doing a bit on California Long White potatoes. Potatoes are quite a Southern staple anyway, so Andy could do a lot with it. He liked the idea and, just based on our little bit of conversation, he decided he would do a funny segment about potatoes the next time he appeared on Perry Como's popular variety show. The bit involved a make-believe phone call about cooking potatoes and Andy pretended that he couldn't hear well while talking to the caller. He repeated "California Long White potato" loudly about four times in his comical way. His humorous skit gave the California Potato Advisory Board a lot of exposure on the very highly-rated "Perry Como Show," and it all started by just putting the "potato" bug in Andy's ear!

Los Angeles newspaper Food Section photo of Andy with turkey and mashed potatoes.

☆ ☆

The Mickey Mouse Race for Potato Publicity

I look back with amazement at the diversity of publicity we used to put California Long White potatoes on the map. For example, the "Mickey Mouse Club" no sooner appeared on the air in 1955 than it quickly grabbed the youth audience of America. It was the first show for young viewers across-the-board; it appealed to both children and teenagers. Unlike early kids' programming, such as "Ding Dong School" and "Captain Kangaroo," the "Mickey Mouse Club" catered to kids as "the leaders of the 20th century," instead of treating children like overgrown babies. This was an important concept; as we all know, children want to be thought of as "grown up" and not associated with anything that is baby-like. In fact, the "Mickey Mouse Club" was reported to have the highest viewership of any show at that time. It appealed to adults, as well, who could share it with their children after school and before dinner, because of the show's opportune air time in the late afternoon.

The show gave me a great opportunity to present my California Long Whites. The Disney studio, where the "Mickey Mouse Club" was filmed, claimed that over 91% of the viewing audience between 5-6 p.m. daily was tuned to the show. So I arranged to have a complete feature about California Long White potatoes appear on the "Mickey Mouse Club" show. With the producers, Lee & Associates created "The Great Potato Race," which was so well done, it ended up as a two-part presentation on the "Mickey Mouse Newsreel." That meant we would get a 10-minute segment presented on two consecutive days. We created a story about a 12-year-old boy from Shasta, California, which is right in the middle of the potato belt. In the script, he had been given a few acres of land to grow potatoes. The newsreel, being education-oriented, showed the harvesting, processing and marketing of potatoes. We covered California Long White potatoes from beginning to end, and as an added bonus, the film gave a strong message about taste and nutrition at the end of the story. (I wonder today how many of those children of the 1950s, who watched the potato newsreels, truly became our "leaders of the 20th century." Hopefully, they still include nutritious potatoes in their healthy diet.)

After the newsreels ran, the potato growers really got excited and were totally impressed with this presentation. We had a big party in Los Angeles at our photographer's studio, utilizing several potato recipes, and many members of the media attended (see next page).

Easy Sloman

. . . MASHED NOTES

ATTENDED, out of sheer curiosity, a peculiar party the other day. It was the only party this department ever heard of that had as its guest of honor a potato.

This party was given in honor of the long white California potato, by the Long White Potato Advisory Board, a quasi-official state organization dedicated to the advancement of the cause of potatoes.

Met a man named Leo Pearlstein, who seemed to be in charge. Found out he WAS in charge. He told me a lot of things about potatoes, then led me to a buffet supper. Potatoes, by golly, in every form you could imagine. Potato dumplings on stew, potato rolls, a dish compounded of potatoes and crabmeat, mashed potatoes, baked potatoes, potato cake, potato pudding.

Sloman

Learned from Mr. Pearlstein that potatoes are a major California crop, that the Advisory Board was established by state law after a majority of the potato growers in California decided they wanted one, and that its function is to get people to eat more potatoes.

Decided there was no time like now, and tried some. They were good to eat.

Big commotion at the door just then distracted me from eating potatoes. Turned out to be Governor Goodwin J. Knight putting in an appearance on behalf of potatoes. People milled around, other people took pictures of the Governor with potatoes and with the people who were milling around.

Somebody asked Mr. Pearlstein why no movie starlets were present. Someone else supplied an answer: just before election time, it's easier to get a politician than it is to get a starlet.

Mr. Pearlstein supplied another answer: in addition to running the Long White Advisory Board, he operates the state's Turkey Advisory Board, and he says the movie people who are in charge of supplying starlets for things like this are leery of him because of his connection with turkeys. People in show business, he said, are very sensitive to turkeys, as a symbol of unsuccessful theatrical enterprise and prefer to leave turkeys and anyone connected with turkeys strictly alone.

Man who has the TV show "Panorama Pacific" was there, looking around to see if long white potatoes would make good material for his program. He turned out to be a potato enthusiast, and supplied Mr. Pearlstein with a dandy recipe for stuffing turkeys with potatoes. Mr. Pearlstein beamed.

There was another big commotion at the door. The Governor was leaving. I didn't get to meet him. Probably just as well. Philip Brown, a Democrat, was daring me to finagle an introduction to him and then say, "Sorry—I didn't get the name." Might have done it, too, just to brighten Goodie's day.

Well, anyway, we should all eat more potatoes.

* * *

Let the sky rain potatoes.
—The Merry Wives of Windsor,
Act 5. scene 5.

Courtesy of The Pasadena Star News

6

Steve Allen, Man For All Seasonings

☆ ☆

Like Groucho Marx, Steve Allen did not know many of his non-celebrity guests until they came out on stage. He was completely unrehearsed when we sent our actresses over to demonstrate a food product on his show. What came out of his mouth was pure improvisational wit, native only to a comedic mind that is always "on." For about a decade, we booked talented young guests on the "Steve Allen Show" who were spokespersons for our clientele. Included were such titles of note as Miss Chives, Miss Peanut, Miss Turkey, Miss Turkey Stuffing, Miss Boysenberry, Miss Apple, Miss National Cranberry, and Miss Sake, among others. You can imagine the fun Steve had with these appellations. It was his style to educate viewers while he was entertaining them, so the sketches we created appealed to him on both levels.

☆ ☆ ☆

Miss Chives, our Carolyn Devore, walked onto the "Steve Allen

Steve and "Miss Chives" (Carolyn Devore) clown around with her crown.

*Is Steve holding a chive,
or is he flashing the
"A-Okay" sign?*

*Steve Allen—original
"King of Late Night TV"
and a prince of a fellow.*

Show" wearing a bathing suit decorated with thousands of chives which had been glued on right before the show to maintain freshness. Steve's jaw dropped as he comically feigned an attempt to censor her scanty attire, barely covered by the tiny greens. He hurriedly put his handkerchief in front of her, but nervously dropped it.

"Don't bend over, I'll pick it up," he said, without missing a beat, as his studio audience roared with laughter, as undoubtedly did millions of his TV viewers.

Then noticing the virtual lawn of chives growing on her swimsuit, Steve ad-libbed:

"You're all broken out—in a case of chives!"

"Yes, I'm from the California Institute of Chives," the blond Miss Chives answered nonchalantly, as if nothing at all was remarkable about the name.

But it caused Steve Allen to convulse in a fit of giggles. "Where is the California Institute of Chives?"

"In California," Miss Chives smilingly answered.

"I mean, there's Disneyland, and MGM, and NBC, and oh, look mother, there's the California Institute of Chives!" Allen imitated a child looking off into the distance while the audience shrieked with laughter.

Later, she had Steve sit down and began serving him a baked potato. Miss Chives discovered that the main ingredient (chives) to sprinkle on top of it, was not on the table. So he began to pick a few off her skimpy bathing suit, all in good taste, of course. She continued on, blithely lecturing about chives, pointing out that many well-known people had eaten them, including Cleopatra. Miss Chives sounded like a history teacher who was very much out of her schoolmarm dress code.

"You know, all the gods of fertility ate chives." she proclaimed.

A mesmerized Steve Allen, looking away from her costume and covering his eyes, muttered in a shuddering voice,

"Never mind the gods of fertility!"

☆ ☆ ☆

Of all the people we worked with in the television industry, Steve Allen was, without a doubt, the brightest. He was also the truest gentleman. I can't say enough in his favor. In addition to his many talents and his graciousness, he certainly educated his viewers through humor. We have always felt education was one of our most important tasks as public relations counselors. Audiences will listen when you make it easy and amusing for them. As you can see from the dialog above, even a simple chat about a little green plant can become a laughing matter. I wonder to this day how many people recall that silly interview from the "Steve Allen Show," when they dive into a baked potato heaped with chives?

How did we come up with these comedic scenarios? We had no formal script. We would simply contact Steve's producers and suggest guests whom we felt would entertain and, at the same time, put in a good, solid message about our products in an educational manner. We expected laughter. In

"Miss Peanut" (Corrine Cole),
extolling peanut virtues to
Steve and his audience.

fact, we worked with the producers to come up with props, themes, and concepts we knew would provoke chuckles. It's easy when your products have a little built-in humor, as mine usually did. Everything else came right off the top of Steve's head while he was on the air. The segments with our food products were so ripe with wit that the producers called us back again and again, knowing we were never at a loss to produce creative ways to serve up fun foods.

We arranged for props, costumes, and lots of food to hand out to the audience. Unlike at our shows, not everyone came to a routine taping of a TV show here in Hollywood and went home with free chives, pretzels, Danish cheese, prunes, turkey stuffing or boysenberries. Let's face it, these aren't your usual freebies.

Steve learns about cooking with tasty prunes.

We would interview up to 10 young women before we chose the spokesperson we wanted, the lady who could be the best "Miss Whatever" to represent the product we were promoting at the time. We chose them for their intelligence and their beauty. We coached our spokespersons at length, to make sure they had enough product information to keep them on the show segment as long as possible. Knowing this, several of the young women did their own research and became quite knowledgeable about the product they represented and the many ways it could be served. Most of all, we wanted to provide a good rapport between Steve and our representatives, so they could have great fun entertaining the audience. In some cases, we were very conservative; in others we went wild, knowing the possible double-entendres would all but stop the show. In every one of our plugs, we received positive on-air messages about our products, and that was the bottom line. To this day, I still get comments on the informative appeal of the "Steve Allen Show" segments we helped create, whenever anyone sees them in reruns or on tape.

Don't think it was all just food jokes. You'd be surprised what we did with some of the products. When Miss Boysenberry (Marilyn Fox) appeared on Steve's show, she presented a tray filled with boysenberry ice cream, boysenberry brandy, a boysenberry and vodka drink, boysenberry sherbet—you name it, we came up with it. Of course, if Steve Allen liked it, so would the whole world.

"Miss Chicken" visiting
Steve's show.

☆ ☆ ☆

Miss Boysenberry handed Steve a snifter of boysenberry brandy that he eagerly tasted.

"That really hits the spot—and it's been a long time since my spot has been hit," he said, licking his lips. Then, after an outburst of audience laughter, she handed him the boysenberry juice drink.

"Well, I'll be dad-blasted—and it's been a long time since my dad has been blasted, too!" Steve took another sip. "Well, I'll be dad-gummed—and it's been a long time since my dad has been gummed!" Steve looked at the camera, as if sharing an ongoing private joke with his audience. "Dad-

burned! Hornswoggled!"

Steve: "Now, what do we have here, a bunch of poker chips?"

Miss Boysenberry: "No, these are little pancakes, if you'd like to try some with boysenberry syrup on them."

Steve folded a pancake over and sopped it up with boysenberry syrup that he dripped all over the place. Then he took a napkin and waved it in the air, pretending to wipe the syrup off viewers' TV screens. The one-liners kept on rolling, as boysenberry juice trickled down his chin and Miss Boysenberry had to quickly daub his face with a napkin to avert a potential mess. Steve apologetically quipped, "I don't want to look a gift berry in the mouth!" But the segment was getting a little too juicy.

Decorum quickly recovered and Miss Boysenberry belted out her vocal rendition of a catchy jingle that the band had rehearsed ahead of time. It was called "The Boysenberry Jam," and she and Steve created a new dance, as well as a new dance team.

☆ ☆ ☆

We almost had a disaster once, though, when we had Miss Turkey walk on stage with a live, rather hefty 60-pound bird that was so huge it waddled. The turkey had traveled into Hollywood from a desert town nearly 50 miles away, and had been tranquilized to keep it calm during the trip. When the turkey walked on stage, Mother Nature took her course, as she is prone to do with animals at the most inopportune moments. The gargantuan bird

Steve cuts up while "Miss California Turkey" (Eve Bruce) does the carving.

began to leave a deposit on the floor, bigger than what one would generally refer to as bird "droppings."

Steve asked, "How much does the turkey weigh?"

Miss Turkey answered, "Sixty pounds."

"Well—more or less," Steve noted, as the bird finished its business while the audience roared.

When things got back to normal, Steve spent several minutes extolling the virtues of turkeys, which was no easy feat after the gales of laughter. He helped bring home our message that turkey is a healthy food and that no one needed to wait until the holidays to eat it. "Anytime is turkey time." It was quite an endorsement for our client, one that simply could not be bought in terms of advertising dollars.

Guess what? The next day the president of the National Turkey Fed-

"Miss California Turkey"
shares some information and a lot of laughs with Steve Allen.

"Crowning around" with "Miss Turkey Stuffin'" (Arlene Charles).

"Miss Turkey Stuffin'" giving Steve some holiday cooking tips.

eration—quite a powerful organization—sent a telegram to the California Turkey Advisory Board (our client), suggesting that the person (yours truly) who arranged for that terrible scene on the "Steve Allen Show" should be fired. Luckily, our California turkey growers were a little more broad-minded and knew the tremendous, positive exposure the turkey industry had received, which encouraged millions of people to eat turkey more often, and they were very pleased with our efforts.

Talking about turkey, let's not forget the stuffing, or dressing, as many people call it. Yes, we represented dressing, too. One should not serve a meat as popular as turkey without the dressing to go with it. We're long since out of the pioneer days when homemakers made their own dressing out of leftover cornbread and biscuits. Today, packaged dressings are easy to prepare, just as tasty and are filled with all kinds of herbs and seasonings. Pardon the wordplay, but you can dress the dressing up any way you want. We represented Mrs. Cubbison's Dressing Mix back then, which is still one of our clients today. We've been promoting that fine product for over 50 years; it is our oldest account. We occasionally added prunes, figs, cranberries and boysenberries to the dressing on many of the shows, to glamorize the recipes and illustrate to homemakers how versatile they can be.

We cast actress Arlene Charles as Miss Turkey Stuffing, who appeared on Steve's show; indubitably, it was one of our more seasoned titles.

☆ ☆ ☆

Steve: "Miss Turkey Stuffing—how did you get this job?"

Miss Turkey Stuffing: "Well, the people from the Turkey Stuffing Board—"

Steve: "Wait a minute. You mean somewhere on the 40th floor of a skyscraper on Madison Avenue, there's a Turkey Stuffing Board? What does your daddy do? He works for the Turkey Stuffing Board. He's in charge of crumbs."

Lee & Associates created the "Turkey Stuffing Board" on behalf of Mrs. Cubbison's, as another way to publicize the dressing brand name.

☆ ☆ ☆

The interviews we provided for the "Steve Allen Show" ran from 10 to 20 minutes long, because of the humor and entertainment they provided. In television variety programs today, such routines are usually given no more than six minutes.

Drinking alcoholic beverages on television was forbidden in those days, like it is now, generally speaking. You might see an actor or entertainer holding an alcoholic drink, but rarely drinking it. Nevertheless, we were able to introduce many such drinks, and even a new liqueur, via a stunt we created, because the "Steve Allen Show" was aired live and viewed later in the evening. The

Guest comic Allen Sherman, "helping" "Miss Sake" (Helen Funai) show Steve a little about Japanese social customs.

interview was tastefully done. We hired lovely Japanese actress Helen Funai as our "Miss Sake," to represent our client, Suntory Whiskey. Helen appeared on the "Steve Allen Show" in what turned out to be a very long segment that included guest comedian Allen Sherman.

Throughout, she was able to introduce several drinks made with Suntory Sake and Suntory Midori Melon Liqueur, with names such as Greensleeves, Pink Cherry Blossom, Far East Sour, Rising Sun and Pink Sayonara.

Steve: "Miss Sake is going to teach you some Japanese customs."

Sherman: "Have you ever been through Japanese customs?"

Steve: (Laughing) "Yes, it takes about two hours!"

Recreating the atmosphere of a Japanese geisha house, Steve strips down to his tee-shirt and pants and lies down comfortably on Japanese floor mats as Miss Sake hands him a cup of warm sake.

Miss Sake: "You don't blow on it, you slurp it."

Steve: "Didn't I see you in a booze ad?"

Miss Sake: "Yes, for Suntory whiskey."

Steve: (Sitting up) "Ooohhhh—in that case, I'm going to tuck in my tee shirt."

Miss Sake then offers Steve two other drinks, one called Greensleeves, made of Suntory Green Tea Liqueur and champagne, and another with Pink Cherry Blossom Liqueur.

Sherman: "What custom is this?"

Steve: "It is called getting stoned."

Sherman: "Now, if you'll lie down on your

Steve doing his hilarious "charming snake" act.

stomach, Miss Sake will massage your back and walk up and down on it Japanese style."

Steve: (Looking incredulous while the audience bellows). "And what will she do if I hang myself from a meat hook?"

The next part of this sequence exhibited such improvisational comedic spirit that today, more than 40 years later, people still burst out laughing when they watch this unrehearsed bit on tape. Miss Sake had Steve slip into a comfortable Japanese kimono designed with a snakeskin pattern. Ironically, Helen had just served him a Japanese hors d'oeuvre made of snake meat. The snakeskin kimono led to one of the funniest improv routines I have ever seen on television. As Steve was donning the robe, he got his left hand caught in the hem of its loose-fitting, ample sleeve. So, arching his covered hand to resemble a snakehead, he wiggled his whole arm in undulating snake moves. It was remarkably lifelike, as good as anything a clever puppeteer could have created. Steve took off with the gag, having a field day. The unprepared cameraman moved every which way, trying to catch the emerging snake-puppet as it sprang to life via Steve's arm and induced gales of laughter from an equally stunned audience.

Steve: "Hellooo, Snakey!" (He writhes the snake-hand toward him.) "What do you have to say to the boys and girls this evening?"

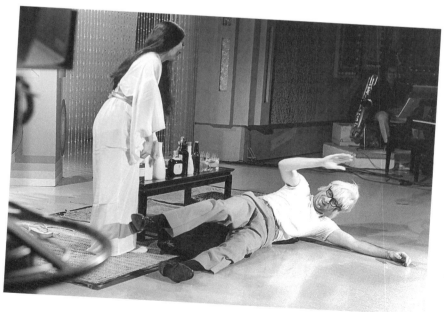

Hey Steve, Allen Sherman said
to lie on your <u>stomach</u> for the Japanese massage!

Helen Funai showing Steve the unusual Suntory bottle.

Snake: (Steve mimics in a high-pitched cartoon-character voice, much like that of Mickey Mouse.)

"I'm stoned—All kidding aside, where's your left hand?"

Steve: "Don't nobody leave the room! My left hand is gone!" Sherman feeds Steve yet another Suntory drink, called the Royal Pagoda.

Steve: "Well, I'll pagoda hell! This is turning into a soiree. Hey, I found my hand!" (Steve finally slides his hand out of the draping sleeve. Helen then hands him a Japanese peanut ball to eat.

Steve: "Have you ever heard, heretofore, of a peanut ball?"

Sherman: (Very deadpan). "Yes, when peanuts get together at the end of the year, they have a Peanut Ball."

Steve: "And some of them really shell out, I'll tell you!"

Helen gives him yet another drink, called the Samurai Sword, and Steve starts to shimmy and sing "Samurai" to the tune of "Summertime." Helen insists the two of them must sip the drink together.

Steve: "The family that drinks together, sings together."

(Steve begins to crack up as he sees an opening to get Helen back for telling him earlier to slurp sake, not blow it.) "Now, if you really want to get the gal loaded, you blow while she drinks!" (Taking a sip). "Well, I declare! Remember her? "I.D. Clare and Her All-Girl Orchestra."

The audience's laughter could barely keep pace with Steve's rapid-fire jokes.

Can you see how we had so much fun

with creating these interviews? We share Steve's "educate and entertain" philosophy, which made for a good match. We could always count on Steve's impulsive eye to find humor in places we didn't realize existed.

☆ ☆ ☆

Miss National Cranberry (Karen Parker) walked on stage carrying a large tray of cranberry drinks.

Steve: "And here we have Miss National Cranberry Sauce or Queen."

Miss Cranberry: "Here's a drink with cranberry juice, vodka and lime."

Steve: "I don't believe that." (Takes a sip.) "I find that very hard to believe." (sip) "Let me see if there's really any vodka in there." (sip) "You must be kidding. A young girl like you wouldn't put vodka in there." (sip)

Miss Cranberry: "Oh, I didn't put it in."

Steve: "Then you didn't take it out either, did you?" (sip) "I just can't believe there's any vodka in there. Let me check that once more." (sip)

With each sip Steve took, the audience laughed louder and longer; escalating when Karen handed him yet another doctored beverage with his name on it.

Miss Cranberry: "Here is another one called the Steverino Smash;

"Miss National Cranberry" (Karen Parker)
pouring a "Steverino Smash" for its namesake.

it has vodka in it, too."

Steve: "Just how long have you been in this cranberry game?"

☆ ☆ ☆

We arranged for the Hollywood Chamber of Commerce to salute Steve Allen in 1990 when Lee & Associates celebrated its 40th year in business. At that function, Bill Welch from the Chamber presented Steve with a plaque that read in part: "The Hollywood Chamber of Commerce salutes this very talented man and his contributions to the world of entertainment. He has, through the years, provided major developments in all areas of entertainment including television, motion pictures, radio, musical composition, live theatre and literature. In television, he developed and presented ideas for the use of this medium that are successfully used by top entertainers today, but were undreamed of before he came on the scene. Probably no single individual has had such an impact on so many aspects of entertainment as has Steve Allen. For what Steve Allen has done to bring humor, happiness and pleasure to the world, the Hollywood Chamber of Commerce expresses its most sincere appreciation."

Accepting the plaque, Steve joked, "I don't think I've ever had so many compliments in one night. I feel as if I've died and, gone to uh, Cleveland. I am indeed honored. As those of you in the advertising and public relations business, and related fields, are aware, there is sometimes a certain commerciality, a certain degree of self-interest in proceedings of this general sort. And I appreciate this specific instance…because there's so much more than that to it."

Leo, Steve Allen and Helen Pearlstein at the Lee & Associates 40th Anniversary event.

☆ ☆

Then he spoke of those years we worked together and explained how those food segments all came together on his show: "One reason I often seemed befuddled in those interviews is because I literally didn't know what was up. Sometimes they (Steve's staff) would warn me if there was going to be something messy done to me. They would come to my dressing room before the show and say 'Wear one of your Hong Kong suits.' Or sometimes they would say 'under-dress,' meaning that my clothes were going to be removed and I should be sure my undergarments would not themselves embarrass me on camera. My stage manager, Johnny Wilson, was the gentleman who always knew what was going on—when I myself did not—and it was he who instigated many of the pranks that befell me."

Steve Allen was as active as ever in his senior years until the day he passed away. He was one of the busiest human beings on the planet. He constantly traveled throughout America and different parts of the world, either performing or hosting an event or receiving another award for one of his many outstanding accomplishments. I am thrilled to have known the man and to have had the immense pleasure of working with him. And I am honored that he took time from his busy life to favor me by writing the foreword to this book.

Part of Steve's many humanitarian activities was as honorary chairman of Parents Television Council in Los Angeles. It is a national group advocating less vulgarity, sex, and violence on television. Steve appealed to parents, grandparents, and families to voice their views to advertisers who sponsor entertainment that causes violent or vulgar behavior.

Steve wrote in Family Circle magazine (September 1, 1999): "This is an issue that concerns Americans all across the political and philosophical spectrum. Citizens on the political right and left, religious believers, nonbelievers and people of all races and ethnic backgrounds are disgusted by a lot of what now passes for entertainment on television. And they can all help to do something about it. You can help to do something about it. The next time you see a program that includes vile and revolting elements, make a note of the station, the network and the advertiser. Then send a brief letter of protest to an executive officer of the company sponsoring the program. Tell these people that you are holding them personally responsible for corrupting the minds and morals of our nation's children. Encourage your friends to write, as well. Appeals to decency and morality may—alas—fall on deaf ears, but if corporations fear marketplace repercussions, I assure you they will pay close attention."

☆ ☆ ☆ ☆ ☆ ☆ ☆ ☆ ☆ ☆ ☆ ☆ ☆ ☆ ☆ ☆ ☆ ☆ ☆

Anyone interested in obtaining more information about this vital programming issue may contact Parents Television Council at 707 Wilshire Blvd., Suite 1950, Los Angeles, CA 90017, or on the Web at: www.parentstv.org.

Steve Allen 1921 - 2000

Steve Allen, a true entertainment icon, passed away on October 30, 2000. He was best known as a pioneer of late-night television, as the first host of "The Tonight Show." He started as a radio disc jockey before launching his TV career in 1953. He wrote thousands of songs, including his most famous one, "This Could Be The Start Of Something Big." He appeared on Broadway and in some films, such as starring in "The Benny Goodman Story" in 1955. He married actress Jayne Meadows in 1962 and the couple had three sons. He passed away at the age of 78. He was finishing his fifty-fourth book.

7

Adventures With Chives

☆ ☆

I could write a whole book just on chives; the versatile little devils can be used on a wide variety of foods. They are tailor-made to be talked about, and therefore yield good publicity. Even Frank Sinatra Jr. could not resist them, as you will see later in this chapter.

Bill Armanino, president of Armanino Farms, was once known as the "Chive King" here in California. We worked with them from the 1960s to the late 1980s, when they sold their farms to McCormick & Co. He then created Arminino Foods of Distinction, which today still produces high-quality frozen pesto and other upscale sauces. When we began working for Bill, most people didn't know what chives were, and the few who did, thought they were green onions. It is a common mistake, even today. In the 1960s, chives were just a cute little onion-fla-vored green herb sprinkled on potatoes and salads. They looked decorative, but I doubt if many people knew they also had flavor. In those days, chives could be lik-ened to a beautiful actress whose looks may overshadow her talent. Chives were not yet fully in the limelight. They were an

There's nothing like a newsletter for corporate promotion.

☆ ☆ ☆ ☆ ☆ ☆ ☆ ☆ ☆ ☆ ☆ ☆ ☆ ☆ ☆ ☆ ☆ ☆ ☆ ☆

"unknown" just waiting for the right promoter to discover them.

Armanino Farms was a family operation run by Guglielmo, his wife Mary and their son Bill. They grew chives and

froze them in little white plastic cups (about the size of a small margarine tub) for the retail market, and froze them in large containers for the huge food service market which catered to quality restaurants and large institutions, such as hospitals. They supplied chives to Kraft Foods, practically putting cottage cheese with chives and sour cream with chives, on the map when these two now-popular items were created. It was our job to promote the frozen chopped chives and later, freeze-dried chopped chives, to the world. Armanino had competitors in the food industry market, but his company provided practically all the frozen and freeze-dried chopped chives in the United States. So we formed the "California Chive Institute" so we could promote them in a noncommercial manner; thus we were able to appeal more to the public by using our various spokespersons. The title may cause a snicker—it got a few laughs on the "Steve Allen Show"—but it had a serious purpose. By creating the institute as an educational source, we could benefit from all activities pertaining to the use of chives. We were considered part of the company's

Bill Armanino (l.) had to get up in the wee early morning hours to make this appearance on TV's "Farm Report."

management and I often traveled to San Francisco to attend board meetings to discuss all phases of marketing. I'll bet when you've seen those jars of chives in the "spices" section of your market, you never knew how much boardroom brainstorming had taken place to draw your attention to them!

An entire public relations study course could be created around this one little green herb, because we used every conceivable means of reaching consumers, retailers, restaurant owners, and industrial users—encouraging them to add chives to their products. First, we did thorough research on chives. For centuries, chives have been used to provide green color and a very subtle flavor to other foods such as soups, salads, sauces, and potatoes. True chives are not green-onion tops. There is no truth to that rumor, although chives look deceptively like tiny green onions. Instead, chives are slender, tubular green leaves that grow in clumps, and they have practically no bulb on the end. A little-known fact is that they are really part of the lily family. However, we call them a cousin to the onion. They have been popular throughout history, and were a favorite of Cleopatra.

Actress Valerie Perrine shows that chives and omelets were made for each other in this publicity photo.

As for subject matter, chives were great to work with. There were all kinds of creative things we could do with them for promotional purposes. Luckily for us, Bill Armanino was the type of client who would cooperate to the fullest when it came to

doing publicity, a great advantage when it comes to getting the media's attention. Recognizing the value of publicity, he encouraged our efforts and worked closely with us. We wanted to take advantage of every opportunity in every area of media exposure that we could afford to pursue: the food editors and food writers of newspapers and magazines, home economists and home economics school teachers, dietitians, chefs, and TV and radio broadcasters—all influentials who could encourage consumers to purchase chives. We also went to trade shows to reach our various target audiences. We demonstrated how to use chives, and we created recipes to go with practically every food known to exist. We even came up with an ad featuring a photograph of an ice-cream sundae with chives on top. Our creative department gave us some pretty strange looks. I suspect they wondered if we were trying to emulate Andy Warhol. Our advertising director looked at me curiously and said, "Chives on sundaes? Did I hear that correctly? Or do you mean 'chives on Sundays?'"

"Chives on sundaes!" I piped up. "And we can add, 'So they don't go with everything, but they do go with potatoes, eggs, soups, and salads.'"

A natural tie-in came with Kraft Foods, well known makers of cheese products. While they had a giant advertising program, we were tiny with no advertising funds, only a small public relations budget. Knowing there was a potential tie-in, I

Baked Potato, chives and sour cream—a great combination.

met with Kraft's public relations and home economics executives, and together we sought out ways to promote their products with chives. We pointed out that during all our promotional activities, we would constantly recommend using chives with sour cream and chives with cottage cheese, and we'd tell people that these products could be bought ready-made. We then exchanged recipes, which to a culinary publicist, is as golden as a handshake! Thus, we all developed an ongoing relationship. As a result, many excellent chive recipes were promoted through the various media. The hearty little green herb soon became a household word and developed a "chive-ly" following!

We also worked with the most popular chefs in the country, especially in Las Vegas, Los Angeles, Chicago, New York, Miami and New Orleans. These major cities are considered "fashion centers" in the food industry. They are excellent for demonstrating new foods and modes of serving them, much like New York and Paris are the centers for clothing styles. We sought tie-ins with hundreds of different food companies and organizations, offering to promote their products generically, if they added chives. This opened a cornucopia of opportunities for us: potatoes, fish, chicken, turkey, rice, soup, salads, and even grapefruit with chives!

We worked with several famous culinary experts to help draw even more attention to the rising popularity of chives, such

International master chef James Beard (l.) and TV master chef Mike Roy discuss chives.

as French Chef Rene Verdon. He was the chef at some of the finest restaurants in France, as well as America. He was also the White House chef for President Kennedy. Celebrities such as Phyllis Diller, Vincent Price, fitness expert Jack La Lanne and many others were cross-promoted with their favorite recipes using chives.

Famous chef, Rene Verdon, using chives in his cooking.

About this time in the early 70s, Frank Sinatra Jr. had recorded an album called "Spice." When we learned he was in Las Vegas, appearing at the Frontier Hotel, we called our friend Hank Kovell, who was considered the dean of the Las Vegas hotel publicists. He handled PR for the Frontier and other Howard Hughes Las Vegas hotels. Hank is a highly skilled professional and very promotion-minded; he even formed a group that consisted of all the downtown Las Vegas hotel publicists. He and I had done several very successful photo tie-in promotions in the past. I told Hank that we wanted to contact Frank Sinatra, Jr., hoping to do a promotion with him at the hotel. Could he arrange a meeting so that we could all talk about it? We had several ideas that we were sure would be mutually beneficial.

Jack La Lanne mentioned using chives in healthy cooking.

Contacting Hank helped a lot, as I found out later; most celebrities are bombarded by people seeking promotions and tie-ins. Unfortunately, many of those promotions never work out, or the publicists make promises and never follow through. Hank spoke up for us, telling Tino Barzi (who was then Frank Jr.'s manager) and

Frank about our previous promotions, relaying that we had a reputation for following through and being very efficient. Also, we had wholesome food accounts that appealed to everybody and could give Frank a new dimension of public relations exposure.

I flew to Las Vegas to meet with Frank Jr., Tino and later with Hank. Together, we worked out promotional tie-ins that lasted as long as a year, and helped everyone concerned. Armanino, in addition to producing chives, had a new product called San Francisco Seasoning, which was sold in small foil packets. We used those and several other items to develop a promotion. First, we created a news release about spice and wove into the story the fact that Frank Sinatra Jr. loved to cook. This tied in perfectly with his new "Spice" album. Sinatra Jr. and San Francisco Seasoning were "a perfect blending" at the time; it was an excellent way to spice-up publicity on both sides. We prepared recipe leaflets featuring chives and the seasoning, including information about the record album. These were sent out to the entertainment media and to selected disc jockeys, to draw attention to this project. We also provided Hank with a supply of spice packets and recipes to have them placed in the guest rooms at the Frontier Hotel.

We created an event to honor Frank Jr. for his cooking and recipes, on behalf of the California Institute of Chives. He even

Frank Sinatra, Jr., "Bachelor Chef of the Year," reads chive recipes during a radio interview.

Frank Jr. (r.) enjoys cooking and has great respect for professional chefs.

referred to it in his stage show. Then we set up a complete photo session in the Frontier's kitchen with Frank Jr. wearing a chef's hat and apron. He was photographed creating recipes and working with the chef. One of the photos was put on the cover of a recipe leaflet, which was all related to Frank Jr., his entertainment company and his newest album. These recipe leaflets were sent throughout the country, via the media and supermarkets, receiving a tremendous amount of distribution.

We also helped create a new format for Frank Jr. to appear on various television shows, presenting him as an entertainer with a newly discovered hobby: cooking! For example, we arranged for him to appear on the "Dinah Shore Show," at which time he did a big cooking segment centered around making pizzas. It was "National Pizza Week" at the time. He used chives, of course, to plug his "Spice" album and his appearances.

Subsequently, we had other photos of Frank Jr. posing with chives and other products. We not only kept our promise to promote Frank Jr. and his album, but went above and beyond the call of duty. Happily, Frank Jr. and our client, Armanino Farms, were very pleased. Frank Sinatra Jr. and Tino Barzi were gracious, cooperative and appreciative. They were very congenial. It was a tremendously successful—and unforgettable—promotion!

I must say, after our hard work, it was very gratifying to have helped a little-known herb achieve culinary stardom.

Frank Jr. shows off his pizza dough tossing prowess to Dinah on her popular daytime show.

8

Salami Sponsors Zsa Zsa Contest — No Baloney

☆ ☆

Introducing Hungarian salami to the United States is truly one of the most interesting promotional projects in which Lee & Associates has ever been involved. Publicity efforts met with spectacular media results. After two years of negotiation with the U.S. Department of Agriculture, Pick Hungarian Salami was able to import their product into America in 1985. Ever since the Cold War began in 1945, Hungarian salami was not allowed into the United States, a period lasting nearly a half century. This was quite a loss to both countries, as Hungary is celebrated for its meats, and Americans love "cold cuts" of dried beef and sausage.

You can see why the importation of Hungarian salami was such a big deal; it also symbolized the end of the Cold War conflict. This project came our way when one of our affiliates, Ruth Morrison, asked us to help her re-introduce the Hungarian salami to Americans. While her agency handled the eastern U.S., our agency would handle the west. Between the two of us, we would also see how many news services we could pick up to fill in major cities in between. Since Lee & Associates is located in Los Angeles—to most people around the country that means Hollywood, show business and movie stars—we wanted to come up with something glitzy that would get a lot of attention for this product, because it had been over 40 years since any "real" Hungarian salami had been available to Americans.

While trying to think of a news hook to draw attention to the Hungarian salami, and wanting to associate Hungary with something glamorous, we came up with Zsa Zsa Gabor. The famous Gabor sisters were probably Hungary's most alluring exports; they included Zsa Zsa and her two prominent sisters, Eva (who starred in the popular 1960s sitcom "Green Acres") and Magda. Plus, Zsa Zsa had been very gifted at attracting news coverage (as well as controversy) for several decades. Her warm, effusive charm and bewitching Hungarian accent have made Zsa Zsa "famous for just being famous," in addition to her eight notable marriages. (Both Zsa Zsa and her sister Magda were married to noted actor George Sanders, at different times, of course.) Known for being "always a bride and never a bridesmaid," Zsa Zsa epitomizes Hollywood glamour with her jewels (supposedly acquired from many male suitors) and stunning wardrobe. Her "rich, famous, and proud of it" show-business personality was infectious. We knew that any promotional tie-in with Zsa Zsa Gabor would get plenty of news coverage. With further brainstorming, Ruth came up with the inspiration of having a Zsa Zsa Gabor look-alike contest.

A national gourmet food show was being held in the huge Los Angeles Convention Center, which provided an opportunity for the Pick importers to introduce the famed Hungarian salami. Fortunately for us, the Variety Arts Theater is located almost directly across the street from the convention center. The theater is a beautifully restored building dedicated to the revival of vaudeville and music from that bygone era; it was the perfect location for our look-alike contest. We would invite the food editors and other media representatives who were covering the gourmet food show; they could walk right over to our event after the food show exhibits were closed for the afternoon. We would also invite the general media to show up for the contest. In a word, our event would attract

*Beautiful Eva Gabor, Zsa Zsa's sister,
achieved her fame starring on TV's "Green Acres" sitcom.*

many different types of good, favorable publicity in one convenient location.

The contest was open to women 18 years or older, who would be judged on their resemblance to the Hungarian-born actress and their ability to duplicate her glamorous accent and style. We even told prospective contestants that wigs were perfectly acceptable; all they had to do was send in a photo so we could get an idea of what they looked like as Zsa Zsa. The prize was well worth any woman's efforts at the impersonation: a week's vacation for two in Budapest, with accommodations in a luxurious hotel overlooking the romantic Danube River. We also created a tie-in with Ron Smith who runs a successful, celebrity look-alike talent agency, here in Hollywood. The winner, as well as the first two runners-up, would get a one year talent contract with Smith, who also agreed to be one of our judges.

We sent out news releases to all the media and news wire services. We were able to promote the product by noting that the contest was part of the celebration surrounding the arrival of the first authentic, imported Hungarian salami in the United States in over 40 years, and it was being sponsored by Pick Hungarian Salami Importers.

Our story was an immediate hit, being picked up by every branch of the media who had great fun speculating about the contest. Many of the headlines were plugs for salami in themselves, such as: "Zsa Zsa Gabor Look-alike Contest Heralds Return of Real Hungarian Salami," "Iron-Curtain Salami Said To Be Imported," and "Three Cheers for Hungary! Their Wonderful Salami is Now Available in U.S." The more amusing headlines read: "Ga-Ga for Zsa Zsa," "Salami is Pick of Pork," "No Baloney: He Wants Zsa Zsa!" "Salami Importer Seeks Zsa Zsa Gabor Double," and "Hungarian Ham."

Zsa Zsa Gabor, being a famous person, is considered in the public domain. Unlike a private citizen, her permission was really not needed to hold a Zsa Zsa Gabor look-alike contest. That said, we certainly did want her participation, if only to lend even more excitement to the contest. We thought it would be a great idea if she would be nice enough to be one of the judges in her own contest. My son, Howard, who was handling most of the arrangements for the event, contacted Miss Gabor through her publicity agent by writing her a personal letter and giving her a formal invitation to be one of the judges. The letter explained how this product from her homeland of Hungary was being introduced into America for the first time in over 40 years. Since she was one of Hungary's most

☆ ☆

famous natives, the promotion of the product, which in essence would draw attention to her native country, also paid tribute to her. The next day, a special delivery letter arrived at the agency addressed to Howard, stating that Miss Gabor wanted nothing to do with this contest and instructed us to cease and desist with the contest, or she would sue the agency, the salami company and anyone associated with this event.

We could not believe that she reacted in this manner. After much thought and consideration, we decided to not use Zsa Zsa's name, but still go on with the promotion. Howard acquired Zsa Zsa's home address and sent a large bouquet of lilacs, which were Hungary's most popular flowers, with an apology explaining that we were still going to do the contest promotion, but without using her name, as she requested. He added that he hoped she would reconsider being one of the judges for the contest.

Another round of news releases went out immediately, explaining how Miss Gabor wanted her name eliminated from the contest, so now it was called the "Miss Hungarian Movie Star Look-Alike Contest." After all, most people would still think of Zsa Zsa Gabor, anyway, when they thought of the only famous Hungarian movie star in America. Well, we received even more media coverage with this angle, because now in addition to being cute, the contest had a little hot controversy associated with it.

We never heard from Miss Gabor again, but we had fun continuing on with the contest. Howard got numerous calls from local newspapers, wire services and radio stations, all wanting to know the inside story of Zsa Zsa and the "Miss Hungarian Movie Star Look-Alike Contest." So, as graciously as possible, Howard told the reporters that, "as per Miss Gabor's wishes, her name would not be used in the contest, even though everyone knew that the contestants would look just like her."

We received numerous entries from quite a variety of women. Most of them, of course, being located in the Hollywood area, were up and coming actresses who saw this as a tremendous opportunity for exposure. Although only a post-office box address was listed for contestants to mail in their entries, a few enterprising Miss Hungarian Movie Star wannabe's figured out how to contact us from the publicity they saw. Our receptionists thought it was fun at first, but then it got to be quite annoying when women called up all day long sounding like Zsa Zsa, purring in the thickest of accents. They asked to speak to Howard, as he was the one being quoted in newspapers and interviewed on radio about the event. The would-be contestants gave their best imitations right on the phone, opening with "Dah-ling, this is Zsa Zsa. Is Howard in?" Many of the affected accents were so good that, if the real Zsa Zsa had actually called us, we would never have been able to tell her from other callers.

The excitement mounted as we got ready for the big event. This was actually fun, even though everyone was under tremendous pressure to get every detail in order.

A PR colleague of ours, Gerry Furth, who specializes in large, special events that include catering, worked closely with us to make sure the hors d'oeuvres we served at the Variety Arts Center were not only extremely creative, but would also utilize the Hungarian salami as much as possible. She introduced us to Roberta Deen, a top caterer who produced 2,000 salami rosettes as hors d'oeuvres. My youngest son, Frank, helped me coordinate the 23 finalists who were lined up backstage, ready for their big moment of glory. They were preparing to do their best Hungarian movie star impersonations, wearing a large variety of gorgeous Zsa Zsa-type gowns, with many sporting a variety of wigs, a la Zsa Zsa. For a contest without Zsa Zsa's blessing, we certainly had a lot of her trooping around backstage.

We hired our good friend Johnny Gilbert, popularly known as the

Johnny Gilbert seeing triple—Zsa Zsas, that is, (l. to r.)
winner, Pat La Pearl, runnerup Helga and second runnerup, Temah Martel.

☆ ☆

announcer for TV's "Jeopardy" game show, to be our master of ceremonies for the Zsa Zsa—oops—Miss Hungarian Movie Star Look-Alike Contest. Appearing ever so dashing in his tuxedo, Johnny introduced the contestants one by one for the judges to make their selection. Our winner was Santa Monica resident Pat La Pearl (don't you just love the name, dahling?) and she looked pretty much like you-know-who. The two dahling runners-up were Temah Martel and a lady known only as "Helga." The three charming women could have created an act among themselves as the Gabor sisters. Hmmm—I wonder if Ron Smith, the celebrity look-alike expert, ever thought of that? Anyway, it was a real class event: with glamorous look-alikes, authentic Hungarian salami hors d'oeuvres, and the spirit of goodwill revived between nations.

A good number of media representatives and leading food executives attended the event and had a great time. The Hungarian salami got some pretty tasty write-ups, too. Zsa Zsa probably got more positive publicity than she had in recent years, due to her many personal controversies, even though she did not want anything to do with our contest promotion. It's too bad she could not have been there; she really would have been the belle of the ball.

The grocery industry was informed about all of the hoopla for authentic, Pick Hungarian Salami and was sent various news releases. As a result of all of the excitement, the retailers bought and featured the salami product with excellent sales results. When it was all over, the media coverage we received was tabulated within a week or two. Not even counting TV and radio exposure, there were nearly 90 million impressions with just the print media alone, for this event. The Pick Hungarian Salami Importers were overwhelmed with such tremendous publicity results.

I was happy Ruth asked us to join her in the project. The real fun is that, in the beginning, when we were all coming up with wild ideas to attract positive media attention, we really didn't know exactly how things would turn out. In this case, we did all the right things and everything worked out extremely well for everyone concerned.

9

A Few New Wrinkles On Prunes

☆ ☆

Selling a sweet and naturally tasty product, such as honey, can be as easy as creating a few buzz words. But selling the public on the many virtues of prunes was a challenge that gave us more than our share of wrinkles.

Every commodity has its attendant group, boards that are formed for research and marketing purposes, to benefit the industry as a whole. Over the decades, I have been involved with over 40 such advisory boards, representing various fruits, vegetables, and meats. The California Prune Advisory Board, a client for over 10 years, was a very hardworking board made up of growers, packers and shippers, all vital to the industry. It was also a very sensitive board. On one hand, its members wanted to sell more prunes, as it represented the tremendous prune crop. On the other hand, they were not very happy when people made fun of

*Jack Webb's "Joe Friday" (r.) discussing the
attributes of prunes with another TV "Dragnet" character.*

☆ ☆ ☆ ☆ ☆ ☆ ☆ ☆ ☆ ☆ ☆ ☆ ☆ ☆ ☆ ☆ ☆ ☆ ☆ ☆

prunes or referred to prunes as "nature's advantage."

The board's advertising agency was desperate to point out the health and nutritional attributes of prunes, as well as their delicious, aromatic taste in its commercials. The comically infamous prune is also a great source of iron, potassium, and Vitamin A. It has no fat and it is low in sodium. But from the publicity point of view, many of the opportunities for promotion would cause comedic banter or discussions about the natural laxative benefits.

Comedian and actor Jack Carter poses with prunes— "the funny fruit."

Prune Humor

Prunes were once considered an "old folks" product, for the "geriatric set" only. We certainly had to reach that very important market of older people, and send them a reminder about the extra health advantages and the great taste of prunes, and give them serving suggestions. If the prune industry was hoping to continue its existence, much less thrive, then it would have to reach younger people, too. As the PR agency for the board, we had to wear two hats—the serious hat and the humorous hat. Why? Because it was necessary to draw attention to the prune by using humor. Then, while the audience or public has some interest, point out the more serious advantages of the fruit. To reach young people, we took advantage of opportunities on television. We had big promotions on "The Dating Game," "What's My Line?," "The Dinah Shore Show," "The Steve Allen Show" and the top Los Angeles teen dance program called, "The Groovy Show."

"What's My Line?" provided us with a terrific opportunity to have some fun and get our client plenty of publicity for prunes in the late 1960s. At the time, "What's My Line?" was probably the hottest show on the air in prime time. This television panel quiz-program was very popular from the 1950s to the 1970s because of its diversified guests. They were people from all walks of life who had unusual, often humorous, occupations. The blindfolded celebrity panel had to guess the occupations from meager clues given to them, a bit like a game of charades.

Here was our golden opportunity to supply "What's My Line?" with an unforgettable segment. We suggested to the producers that we had a perfect guest, Karen Lindsey, as "Miss California Prune." Actually, Karen

"Miss California Prune" (Karen Lindsey) tempts Tony Randall —with what else?—a prune.

had many titles. She was a bright, attractive, wholesome model/actress we had met when she was queen of the Los Angeles Press Club. We hired her on many occasions and considered Karen as one of our team. She eventually became our "Miss Everything," so to speak. We had her as our spokesperson on radio and TV as Miss Peach, Miss Plum, Miss Potato, Miss Egg, "Miss" Mrs. Cubbison's Stuffing, and many others. She didn't actually win all those titles; they were more or less honorary, you could say. But she well-earned them; she studied her subject matter and became well versed on nutrition, menus, recipes,

and the folklore and history of the various products.

The producers of "What's My Line?" decided she would be a good bet. Although we were seeking a plug for prunes, they wanted to be sure that our segment would

Jimmy Durante and prunes.

be funny, informative, and entertaining. We all gathered at my home—Karen, my wife, Helen, and I—trying to come up with subject matter that would keep the producers happy. We had to create a story about how Karen became Miss Prune. Basically there was a "contest" and we chose her as the best of all the models and actresses we knew. Helen then came up with a great one-liner; "Karen, why don't you just say that you won the title of Miss Prune by a process of elimination?" A few seconds later, the almost-subtle humor had us all rolling on the floor with laughter.

Needless to say, the show's panelists, which included Soupy Sales and Arlene Francis, had a ball asking Karen questions about prunes. When Arlene Frances asked the grand question, how had she been chosen Miss Prune, Karen's ready answer brought the house down.

We were sure that our client, the sensitive prune growers, would be upset with that reaction. So we had pre-arranged with the "What's My Line?" producers that Karen also be allowed to talk about the prune's other virtues for two or three minutes, and we just knew that would please the prune growers to no end—it was like getting a free commercial worth hundreds of thousands of dollars. Arlene Francis asked Miss Prune how she got such a beautiful complexion. That gave Karen an opening to say, "Why, by eating prunes of course. Prunes are high in iron, vitamin A, and all sorts of nutrients." This is how we were able to present the serious side of prunes with the humorous.

We were on a roll and, wanting to take advantage of our national exposure, we immediately contacted our producer friends at Dinah Shore's show, "Dinah!," in March of 1975 to suggest the appearance of our successful guest, Miss Prune. Dinah was famous for her cooking segments. At the same time, we contacted comedian Ronnie Schell, known for being very health conscious. Ironically, he had appeared on the Dinah show that very week, talking about his approach to nutrition, as he strongly believes in eating fresh and dried fruits and fresh vegetables. He did a whole comedy bit on her show, using a blender to create "Ronnie Schell's Breakfast in a Blender" (see recipe in chapter 22). It includes blueberries, strawberries, mango, peanut butter and prunes. When Dinah's other guest, Phyllis Diller, drank it on the show, she made a prune face and exclaimed, "Why does it stick to the roof of my mouth?," to which Ronnie quipped, "If the prunes start you, the peanut butter will stop you." The audience howled.

We came up with the idea of giving Ronnie an award on an upcoming "Dinah!" show, and having Miss Prune present it to him. How many people can say they've been given the "Golden Prune Award?" We took

Comedian Ronnie Schell whips up his "Breakfast in a Blender."

☆ ☆

a real prune, sprayed it with gold paint and affixed it to a little plaque engraved, "To Ronnie Schell, The Golden Prune Award, for drawing attention to good nutrition through humor."

We arranged for Ronnie and Karen to appear on the show about two weeks later, so Karen could make the presentation. Ronnie graciously accepted and told Dinah it was the first award he had ever won. With his usual dry wit, he acknowledged that "prunes have an affect on all of us." He brought down the house with, "This is certainly the most moving award I have ever received. I guess this makes me one of your most regular guests," he stated.

That turned out to be an uproarious show. We distributed prunes to the audience who, of course, were delighted with the freebie fruit samples and howled with laughter during the segment. Dinah Shore formally introduced Karen who, by the way, was dressed in a beautiful and elegant, long evening gown, with a sash that read "Miss California Prune." We did not present her as the bathing-suit-beauty type, then commonly used by many publicists. In a very serious manner, Karen presented the award to Ronnie Schell. Ronnie, being fast on his feet, started firing funny questions. One of them was "How did you become Miss Prune?" Karen gave her very hilarious answer with a very straight

"Miss California Prune" (Karen Lindsey), trades prune quips while presenting The Golden Prune Award to comedian Ronnie Schell, as Dinah stifles her laughter.

face: "Through a process of elimination." That started a barrage of prune jibes. Every conceivable double-meaning joke spewed from his lips. Here are a couple of samples:

Ronnie: "How long have you held that title?"

Miss Prune: "Three years."

Ronnie: "Then, I guess that's a running title."

Miss Prune: "You know, Ronnie, everyone in the audience has received a box of prunes."

Ronnie: "I wish you had waited till my part was over before you handed them out."

The laughter was tremendous and the plug lasted for several minutes. Dinah very graciously went over to Karen and announced that she loves prunes, eats them all the time and uses them in her cooking. Her impeccably-timed statement took the audience's attention over to the serious side of prunes. She noted how healthy prunes are, which of course, gave Karen an opportunity to get her plug in about iron, vitamin A, minerals, good taste, and so on.

We were ecstatic. At that time, you couldn't have paid for that kind of advertising. You couldn't have hired someone as well-trusted and influential as Dinah Shore to endorse your product. Again, we got loads of humor, but we secured many good, serious placements, too.

Jeans and Jackets

Now and then in the public relations business, serendipity strikes and a single opportunity can turn into a year-long run-

Phyllis Diller—she can get a laugh out of anything— including prunes.

150,000 leaflets, many with winning numbers, were given out to consumers.

ning publicity campaign. Not only can that add to one's financial security and sense of self-worth, it is exciting to keep the creative juices flowing for that long and see the fruits of your labor affect public opinion. One such experience happened when we saw an ad in a trade journal drawing attention to "Do-Nothing Sedgefield," a revolutionary brand of preshrunk, "sanfor-set," wrinkle-free jeans that had just come on the market at that time, in the early 1970s. The ad mentioned that the jeans didn't wrinkle like prunes. The wrinkles were taken out by a new method of pre-shrinking the fabric; through this process, Sedgefield set the fashion for jeans that year.

We tracked the Sedgefield marketing department down in New York and found out that it was planning a campaign incredibly favorable to prunes, called "Eat Prunes, Don't Wear Them." What a stroke of luck for us and the uptight Prune Board. Because the Sedgefield jeans were not wrinkled, they were the "in thing" to wear. The company was planning a massive advertising campaign, including TV commercials, newspaper ads, and general publicity. They also had the support of the Cotton Council in a national promotional campaign.

You can always tell when anyone in this business is on the ball by calling and saying you'd like to talk to them about doing a "promotional tie-in." If they're smart, they get right with the program instead of saying "send me a letter." For the unenlightened, a promotional tie-in involves incorporating another's publicity into your own, and vice versa, so that both parties get double exposure. It is like "double your pleasure," and also, the price is right: it is a mutual trade-out. One such particular young lady who was on the ball was Madeline Zuckerman, the public relations executive for the Sedgefield "Eat Prunes, Don't Wear Them" jeans campaign. We told her that we represented the prune industry and we could help them promote their jeans. As they were already promoting prunes anyway, could we get together? They were planning to have a press kick-off, utilizing actresses and models wearing their jeans with lots of hoopla. We took our famous Miss Prune to meet with them, and we familiarized their spokespersons with the prune's "best kept secret," its little-known considerable nutritional attributes.

The T-shirt that became ten-thousand walking billboards.

We promised to go all-out with our own radio and TV promotions, and include stories about their jeans. We offered prunes and Sedgefield jeans as prizes for special events and together we created a promotion that got tremendous national coverage. First Prize was "An Almost Lifetime Supply of California Prunes, The funny Fruit"—four cases weighing a total of 96 pounds. That's a lifetime supply for most people, but just a year's supply if you really need a lot of prunes.

We even staged prune giveaways at leading department stores in selected cities nationwide. We hired young men and

35,000 large badges were distributed to the prune faithful.

women models to wear the jeans and hand out prunes to customers as they walked into the stores, telling shoppers,

"Go over and take a look at the new Sedgefield 'wrinkle-free jeans.' We want you to eat prunes, not wear them."

In publicity releases, we jointly covered the nation's news with "The Funny Fruit," with such headlines as: "A New Wrinkle In Snacks" and "Taking The Pucker Out Of Pants."

We also participated in the huge men's apparel trade show that took place in Las Vegas every year. The jeans were the hit of the show and we supplied our Miss Prune to appear in Sedgefield's exhibit, wearing the jeans and handing out prunes, of course. A good and successful time was truly had by all, and we experienced "runs" on both of our products, which is a good thing no matter how you interpret that.

From the little acorn grows the giant oak tree. For us, a seedling idea that sparked when we saw a trade journal ad, grew into a major healthy crop of publicity that didn't need any "pruning" at all.

10,000 bumper stickers gave our promotion even more exposure.

☆ ☆

The Funny Fruit

As I mentioned at the beginning of this chapter, the prune growers didn't have much of a sense of humor about their product, but I guess they must have grown a thicker skin along the way. They were gradually becoming adjusted to the fact that humor sells. Before long, in the 1970s, their advertising agency—Foote, Cone and Belding, in San Francisco—came up with a very clever idea to promote prunes as the "funny fruit that's good for you." Even though they had one heck of a time convincing the Prune Board to do it, the prune growers became less uptight about it and finally gave their consent. The board actually authorized nearly a million dollars to test radio commercials in eight major cities to very aggressively promote this concept.

The Smothers brothers, famed TV and nightclub comedy team, record prune "funny fruit" radio commercial.

The advertising agency hired major comedy talents to do the commercials, all of whom were very popular at the time: the Smothers Brothers, Bob & Ray, Joan Rivers and Burns & Schreiber. The idea was to be funny at first, to get the listener's attention. Then, end the commercial on a serious note, offering nutritional information. We were given the task of providing the advertising agency with the serious information about prunes, with the help of our dietitians and our doctors. We publicized this both to the consumers and to the grocery industry trade publications. We attended the recording sessions so we could photograph each of

Joan Rivers demonstrates her personal prune eating technique.

The comedy team, Bob & Ray garnered The Golden Prune Award.

the personalities.

We did "open-end interviews" with each performer. An open-end interview is one that is pre-recorded with an announcer asking the questions. When the interviews are sent out to radio stations around the country, the announcer's voice has been edited out. By this method, each radio station can then insert its own favorite on-air personality's voice asking the questions that have already been pre-answered by each performer. We had the comedians talk about their funny and serious interpretation of the prune commercial. This other exposure, in addition to their own appearances in the commercial, brought in numerous and amusing free plugs for the prune growers, separate from the paid advertising. It was a fun project, everyone cooperated, and we had lots of positive exposure for prunes.

Guess what? In the eight targeted-market cities where the advertising was tested, sales were up as high as 22%. That's pretty amazing for prunes which, in show-biz terms, were thought to be dried up. The "funny fruit" was on the comeback trail. But believe it or not, some members of the Prune Board who didn't like the commercial idea decided not to continue on with the campaign, even though sales were up! This was close to "the beginning of the end" when the board members did not even get along with each other.

The advertising agency eventually lost the account. But for about another year, we continued doing the pub-

Comedy team, Burns (r.) & Schreiber doing their thing on radio for prunes— "the funny fruit."

☆ ☆

licity until the board disbanded. It was a good thing the Prune Board kept us on for the extra year, because we were able to at least set the stage for ongoing prune awareness after the board met its demise. The members soon rediscovered the necessity of promotion and re-established the board a few years later. When that occurred, we did not try to get the account back. Although it was just our luck that the PR agency that did get the account received a much larger budget to work with than the one we had been given in previous years.

Here's an interesting footnote to the California Prune Advisory Board's obsession with the generic name of their beloved product. In mid-2000, they successfully petitioned the U.S. Department of Agriculture to officially change the name of its fruit from "prune" to "dried plum." Go figure!

Actress Jo Ann Pflug shows that you can like prunes without looking like one.

Frank Gorshin poses with prunes and a delicious use of them.

French actress Danielle Cottet ("Miss Prune Whip") promoted prunes in general and brought attention to the California-grown French variety of prunes. Here, she's appearing on Steve Allen's TV show.

10

Doris Day Gives Pretzels A New Twist

☆ ☆

Doris Day and Rock Hudson were at the height of their popularity in the early 1960s, as one of America's favorite romantic-comedy box-office teams. Their classy, clean-cut, devilishly flirtatious style added a new dimension to the game of romantic love. Audiences couldn't get enough of them, especially when they were joined by popular comedian Tony Randall, who played Hudson's sarcastic, arch-rival for Doris' affections in the 1960s highly successful film "Pillow Talk." Randall also provided his great brand of pessimistic comedy relief in Day and Hudson's second film in 1961, "Lover Come Back."

In 1964, Universal Studios united this popular trio for another romantic-comedy venture called "Send Me No Flowers." We knew one of the prop men who was working on the film and as we represented a well known brand of pretzels, we sent over a few bags of the Rold Gold pretzels to possibly be used in any of the background shots. He called us and asked if we could also get some milk bottles for him to use as a prop. It would have been easier for him to go to the grocery store and get a couple bottles of milk, but it was fine with us that he didn't. In addition to the pretzels, we represented a California company called Alta Dena Dairies. So, we arranged

We placed our Rold Gold client's pretzels in a couple of popular Doris Day movies.

to deliver Alta Dena bottled milk. It appeared in a close-up scene in which Doris Day was holding a large shopping bag full of groceries. The Rold Gold pretzels appeared very prominently, too, when they were caught on camera sticking out of the top of the bag. We did not know about this terrific mass exposure until one of our friends, who saw the movie, called and congratulated us. The moral to this story is that it often pays to make the extra effort and time to hand-deliver the goods. Had we been "too busy," the prop man might have picked up another brand of milk at the corner market, and Alta Dena Dairies would have missed an opportunity of a lifetime. The added plus is that our unexpected plugs for milk and pretzels are still in reruns! Look for our clients' products the next time you see "Send Me No Flowers."

Being very elated, we confidently drove out to Universal Studios to ask their publicity department if we could have a still photo of that grocery bag scene to use for a trade-publicity story; we wanted to send it out to the trade magazines that catered to the grocery store chains. The publicity staff at Universal Studios told us, "It's okay with us if it's okay with Doris Day." Covering all bases, I both called and wrote to Doris Day's office for permission to publicize the still photo from her film. It was a very busy time and, for whatever reason, her office never got back to us. I personally called once a week, every week, from November of 1964 through March of 1965, with no response. "I'll let you know, I'll let you know," is the only reply I received.

In March of 1965, we discovered that Doris Day was leaving for Paris to film a new movie, "Do Not Disturb," for 20th Century Fox studios. Worried that we were not going to connect with her, we called the publicist at 20th Century Fox and told him about our desire to reach Doris Day, but once again we had no luck getting to her. So we suggested if we could get her to okay our publicity photo—which was by now almost stale, but still usable—we would help him promote Doris' latest movie.

With the publicist's help, on the very day before Doris Day was leaving for her extensive stay in Europe, we reached her and asked her to give approval to Rogers and Cowan, her publicity firm. Warren Cowan signed a release on behalf of Doris Day, so that we could use the photo from "Send Me No Flowers." Persistence finally did pay off, even if it took five months. In fact, patience and persistence more than paid off. It gave us the potential for additional positive exposure of our products by helping publicize yet another Doris Day film that was bound to be a hit.

To keep our promise, we agreed with 20th Century Fox to create a mass-mailing project in which we would send pretzels and publicity material to 100 of the leading movie columnists in the country with a note reading, "Do not disturb, these are delicate pretzels. Doris Day loves pretzels. We are sending you these pretzels to enjoy, too." For added excitement, we were able to have our clients come down to 20th Century Fox later, meet Doris Day in person and take photos with her.

In the publicity business, one good turn (or twist) deserves another. To our client's advantage, we got their pretzels to Doris Day. To the studio's advantage, we helped publicize her movies with product placements (Chapter 17 highlights more product placement and tie-in stories). Also, for several years after, we sent her pretzels to munch on at her office. We also sent her chocolate-covered pretzels near the holidays. Movie columnists subsequently wrote about Doris Day enjoying pretzels. Everybody wins!

Another way we promoted Rold Gold pretzels (see page 155).

11

Bob Hope — A Classic

☆ ☆

Promotional tie-ins bring together people and events that we would not necessarily associate as kindred spirits, such as Bob Hope with grapefruits, for example. As I previously mentioned, a "tie-in" basically is a business situation of, "I can help you with this, if you can help me with that." It's a strategic partnership. Socially, it can open up a world of fun, and open the door to new contacts. Among our many produce accounts, we represented grapefruit. To be precise, we handled public relations for the Coachella Valley grapefruit growers, which operated under the name of the California Grapefruit Advisory Board. The name "Coachella Valley" may not strike a chord with too many people outside Southern California, but the territory includes the glamorous turf of Hollywood's most classic celebrities—Palm Springs, and Bob Hope is one of the city's most prominent figures.

The classy Mr. Hope, checking out the grapefruits.

☆ ☆

Our mission with the grapefruit board was to draw attention to the sweet and tangy California grapefruit. Our main competitors were Florida, which is far better known for its citrus than California, and Texas, which has the reputation of growing everything bigger and better. Getting the nation to acknowledge the fine grapefruit crop that exists beyond the Louisiana Territory would require some imagination and ballyhooing on our part.

We did the usual product publicity, sending out a great deal of information about nutrition and taste and offering menu serving suggestions. Because we knew that the name "Palm Springs" had much greater appeal than "Coachella," we wanted to find a way to draw attention to the fact that California grapefruit grows near this glamorous desert city that is almost mythical in people's minds. One of the major events held in Palm Springs every year is the popular Bob Hope Desert Classic Golf Tournament. It is a favorite with Hope who invests a lot of his time, energy and interest in bringing together major golfing pros and celebrities to appear at the five-day charitable sports event, which is the largest golf tournament of them all. The golf classic attracts people from around the

Arnold Palmer, all-time golf great, enjoys Bob Hope's charity tournament, the comaraderie, and visiting with the Coachella Valley Grapefruit Girls.

world, and benefits such worthy institutions as the Eisenhower Medical Center near Palm Springs. So, we spoke to Frank Lieberman, Bob's publicity agent, and suggested that, through our contacts, we could draw attention to the golf classic, the charity and all of the good things that it was doing—from an entirely different angle. We were promoting Coachella Valley grapefruit; we weren't show biz folk and we weren't in the sports world. All we wanted was permission to take publicity photographs at the event, ones that we could use in our joint promotional endeavors, and get a favorite recipe of Bob Hope's that would include California grapefruit. It was a perfect marriage. It worked so well, we would be invited back to the spectacular golf tournament for the next several years.

A-one, and a-two— Laurence Welk counting girls—definitely not his golf handicap!

Just before the Bob Hope Classic each year, we followed through with our part by sending out news releases to food editors and sports editors drawing attention to this great event, and we referred to Bob Hope's favorite grapefruit recipe (see Chapter 22). On the actual day of the Classic, we had our lovely spokespersons, who were young, attractive, models—wear bright yellow tee-shirts that read "I'm a Coachella grapefruit lover." Corny as it

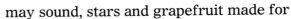

may sound, stars and grapefruit made for a funny and entertaining combination. Even Bob Hope always took time out to pose for us at the event.

Andy Williams relaxed and ready to swing.

We were always as unobtrusive as possible, whenever doing an event, not wanting to cause any overt distraction from the main action. Karen Lindsey, our perennial "Miss Everything," was a very good spokesperson who was able to chat up our grapefruit to the celebrities. Thanks to Bob Hope and the great desert resort location, it almost became a grapefruit festival. In fact, it did add a little glamour, color and fun. The photo opportunities were tremendous, and with the national TV coverage and many of the fan magazines represented there, the celebrities posing with our models and California grapefruit got tremendous exposure.

One of the many country club chefs who served grapefruit to tournament participants had a photo op with our spokeswomen.

My son, Howard, was occupied with asking the various celebrities to pose with our Grapefruit Girls and the fruit. Behind him, thousands of spectators had been cordoned off by ropes (the public was as celebrity crazy in the '60s and '70s as today). Inside the ropes, hundreds of media people from around the world were gathered, all angling for an exclusive interview or photo with the celebrities.

Howard was always among the representatives from such powerful media as the Associated Press, United Press International and Sports Illustrated, and only a few feet away were world-renowned public figures. He had obtained, through channels, the passes that allowed him and the Grapefruit Girls to be close to the celebrities. He was eagerly taking photos, and during the day had secured the cooperation of many name stars.

The never-bashful Mac Davis giving the Grapefruit Girls a friendly squeeze.

Upwards of 20 to 25 well-known entertainers and golf pros came by, including Jack Lemmon, George Peppard, Mac Davis, Telly Savalas, Sammy Davis, Jr., Jack Nicklaus and Arnold Palmer. Howard asked them all to pose; most of these seasoned entertainers had no problem giving out an easy "yes," understanding that it was all in fun, all for charity, and a boon to their own publicity as well, which never hurts any show-biz career, no matter how big.

One year, Howard ran into an interesting predicament. Former President Gerald Ford was in a foursome with Bob Hope, golf pro Johnny Miller, and David Eisenhower, the former president's son. All of them were tightly ringed by Secret Service men who—in the 90-degree

Sammy Davis, Jr., teeing off on "the world's biggest golf ball."

heat—were hardly inconspicuous in their dark glasses, black suit-and-tie and white shirt uniform, the personification of the "men in black" stereotype. Howard was just setting up another group photo with the Grapefruit Girls and a Hollywood celebrity, when he spotted President Ford. He started walking toward the president with the idea of getting a good shot of him. But apparently, the Secret Service men were wondering exactly what kind of shot Howard was planning on. A couple of the more burly agents quickly stopped him, one of them actually thrusting his arm out and blocking Howard in the chest, to the point that it stunned him. The Secret Service man then officiously asked him, "What are you doing?" even though it was obvious Howard had a press badge and a camera.

President Ford and the Grape-fruit Girls—that's Howard Pearl-stein (r.) setting up the photo.

We had a little bit of a scary situation on our hands. They were wondering, "Who the heck is this guy, trying to set up a photo of the President?" Fortunately, President Ford recognized Howard from our attendance at the golf classic during previous years, and with a smile on his face, he waved him over. We had taken his photo before.

"How's your golf game going today, Mr. President?" Howard asked.

"Ah, just great, but let's take a break for

the photo," President Ford said. "I want to be in the picture with all these pretty girls and their California grapefruit." What a politician!

As it happened, probably 30 or more of the many photographers covering this event were at this same location around the ninth hole. They had literally come from around the world to attend this important sports event, which was sprinkled with top celebrities throughout. The photographers also began shooting photos of President Ford and Bob Hope with the "grapefruit girls." Our photo setup caused so many flashbulbs to go off, you might have thought strobe lights had been installed on the golf course. Luckily for us, our California grapefruit were seen around the world through the various local and national press. It was tremendous press exposure.

Jack Nicklaus—the "Golden Bear" and the "golden girls" of grapefruit.

Howard and I got a kick out of how the various celebrities were dressed, especially President Ford who wore white pants with tiny black squares on them. The checkered pattern in his pants turned out to be miniature caricature silhouettes of Bob Hope with an exaggerated ski-slope nose. The ever-gracious Jack Lemmon always wore a bright, lemon-yellow colored sweater. We had fun with the caption on his photo, which read, "Lemmon Pairs with Grapefruit!" Andy Williams, always dapper in his collegiate dress style, usually wore a sky blue sweater and cream colored pants. There was a variety of funny shaped hats and also wild patterned pants and shirts in many colors.

I look back on these events with many memories of a classy and classic fellow, Mr. Bob Hope. I applaud the continuing fine work and many benefits derived from his charity golf tournament.

Baseball great, Johnny Bench

TV's "Kojack," Telly Savalas

TV talk show host, Mike Douglas

Comic Flip Wilson

12

Cooking In The Kitchen With Dinah

☆ ☆

One of the most successful TV show segments we ever helped create was on the popular daytime "Dinah!" show in the 1970s. We could have given it the title, "The Dinah Omelet Show." We flew cooking "eggspert" Howard Helmer out from New York and presented him to Dinah's producers as the "World's Fastest Omelet Maker," as he was listed in the Guinness Book of World Records. With all his vast eggs-perience, he could cook up a whopping 427 omelets in a mere 30 minutes. His goal was to teach Dinah's all-star guests how to whip up a perfect omelet in about 30 seconds. This time, our client was the California Egg Council, while Helmer, one of our agency affiliates, represented the huge American Egg Board as his client.

We proposed to Dinah Shore's production staff that we would handle everything for the segment; they would not have to worry about labor and costs. We arranged for the equipment, the stove, pots and pans, dishes, utensils, and all the food. It paid off because, boy, did we get a

Howard Helmer (far l.), shows (l. to r.) James Stewart,
Steve Laurence, Dinah, Eydie Gormé and Lucille Ball, the fine art of omelet-making.

lucky break that day! Dinah had a lineup of guests who just happened to be among Hollywood's top royalty: Jimmy Stewart and his wife Gloria, Steve Lawrence and Eydie Gormé, Lucille Ball and her husband, producer Gary Morton.

Each guest was provided with an omelet pan, and Howard Helmer's job was to teach them all, including Dinah, how to make 30-second omelets. Talk about "cooking in the kitchen with Dinah," we really had a stellar team going gangbusters, flipping fluffy omelets.

Sounds simple enough. The fun started when we provided a whole array of ingredients for them to include in their omelets, which turned the elementary cooking lesson into a comedy routine. Martha Stewart should get so lucky. From a public relations standpoint, we had an uproarious success. The viewers were not only entertained, but they saw how easily, quickly and creatively omelets could be made, not to mention that the viewing audience had a prominent culinary instructor and "star" pupils from which to learn. The tremendous variety of ingredients we

Dinah Shore, "America's Sweetheart," receiving the "Good Egg Award" from Dean Olson, Chairman of the Califorua Egg Council.

provided conveyed the idea that viewers could have an omelet party on their next social occasion. To maximize the effectiveness of the segment for us, we included all of our appropriate clients, such as chives, various frozen foods and cheeses. We also provided artichokes, even though we didn't have the artichoke board as a client, yet. We were pitching that account the following week, so we got them a free plug on this popular national TV show. Incidentally, we got the account (this event probably helped)!

The segment ran over the allotted 15 minutes; in fact, we got an extra two minutes. That's a lot of air time for positive national exposure of our clients' products. The producers were so pleased that they repeated the show at another date.

This show segment is a perfect example of the value of public relations. We entertained and educated, we had celebrities using our products, and we were on stations around the country on this tremendously high-rated show. Plus, we got permission from the show's producer to take photos of the event, which we were able to use as part of our ongoing egg promotion. Of course, the Egg Council was very pleased.

Another Date With Dinah

One other segment we did for the "Dinah!" show included our client Suntory International, a billion-dollar Japanese conglomerate that produces over 100 different beverages, mostly alcoholic. We represented Suntory Whiskey and several of the company's wines. When they introduced a new product, Midori Melon Liqueur, we wanted to do something spectacular. We knew that if we could get exposure on the "Dinah!" show, that would really get our client excited. Howard contacted the producer and told her we wanted to have the very first case of Midori Melon Liqueur delivered directly from the Japanese ship to the "Dinah" stage at CBS studios in Hollywood, just as soon as it arrived. Dinah and her guests would have the first taste of this new liqueur, which was being introduced in America.

He told the producer we could create a segment with a Japanese theme to highlight the product, including props and a Japanese actress to serve the Midori Melon Liqueur (again, we provided everything, saving the studio labor and costs). The producer liked the idea and said she would discuss it with the executive producer. If they felt that it was appropriate for the show, they would get back to us. As the Midori shipment would actually arrive in America about six weeks later, Howard hoped to hear back from the producer prior to the liqueur's grand entrance into the United States. We got down to the wire, and were on pins-and-needles waiting. About five weeks passed since Howard heard anything when finally, he received a call from the producer one afternoon. As it turned out, the timing was perfect for the coming week's show, since one of the guests would be Ed McMahon, the famous sidekick of late-night talk show favorite, Johnny Carson. Ed's image was that of a man who has enjoyed a drink or two from time to time, even though he didn't actually drink as much as everyone joked about. The other guest scheduled to be on the show for that day was Richard Thomas, famous for his role at that time as John Boy in "The Waltons" TV series. Thomas had a very squeaky clean, home-spun image. If they could drink the melon liqueur, then it would convey a positive message to the public that the liqueur was a classy, after-dinner drink.

"Miss Sake" (Helen Funai, r.) introducing Suntory's new melon liqueur to Ed McMahon, Dinah and America.

Even more fantastic for us, the producer wanted to fill two segments—that's about half an hour. She even asked Howard to include other products and arrange for our spokesperson to tell about their history in relation to Japanese culture and custom. I contacted lovely Japanese actress Helen Funai, who had a recurring role in one of the popular daytime soap operas. Helen had appeared as our spokesperson on other shows, such as Steve Allen's, so I arranged for her to be on Dinah's show, as well, in full Japanese kimono costume. Howard worked with the prop director and set designer to arrange to have authentic Japanese items placed around the set for a sense of atmosphere.

During the commercial break, before Helen was introduced, Dinah, Ed McMahon, and Richard Thomas all got into the act by donning kimonos, as well. When the show came back on, Dinah began asking Helen about ancient Japanese customs, especially one concerning backrubs. The producer had prearranged with Ed McMahon to volunteer for Helen's Japanese-style backrub. What Ed didn't know is that this type of backrub, known as shiatsu massage, included having Helen walk across his back. Ed was rather stunned when Helen told him on the air. Well, the audience went wild! Ed was asked to lie down on a floor mat, and then she took off her shoes and walked up and down his back. It was hardly what one would call a relaxing experience for him, but it was all in fun.

After that, Dinah suggested they try a little something else to relax them. I think the visibly shaken Ed, with his exaggerated interest in alcohol, was more than ready for that. Here was the moment we had been waiting for, our grand opportunity to introduce the new Midori Melon Liqueur. Dinah—in her warm, easy and informative pretty schoolmarm way—explained to Ed and Richard that they were having the first taste of this new liqueur imported into America. Normally, alcohol was never consumed on a "live" TV show, so this was really a first on a network show. We had arranged for Helen to discuss the ancient ritual of drinking sake and to plug Suntory's sake product, in addition to the company's very popular Suntory Royale Whiskey.

What pleased us tremendously is that we got many close-ups of the products and their Suntory labels. Ed commented that the liqueur was absolutely delicious and Richard said he enjoyed it, as well. The ever suave Dinah Shore told the nation how much she enjoyed the products and thanked Helen for coming on the show with them. This plug was worth a million bucks with endorsements from these people—Ed McMahon, from one of the most popular late-night talk shows ever, "The Johnny Carson Show;" Dinah Shore, "America's Sweetheart;" and Richard Thomas, who had one of the purest images on television.

All of us at Lee & Associates were extremely excited and pleased with the way things went. I happily called the client and told the executives to watch this spectacular segment a couple of days later when it would air around the country. After the show was over, I received many congratulatory phone calls from public relations friends and colleagues. They

☆ ☆

knew how difficult it was to plug alcohol on television and that this was a fantastic publicity coup. But, interestingly enough, no phone calls of congratulations came from the client. So, I called the marketing director a couple days after the show aired, and asked what he thought of the segment. The client mildly replied, "It was very nice." It turns out that the Japanese people do not express themselves as openly as Americans do. While they certainly appreciated the exposure, they did not express themselves to the agency anywhere near the way our other clients would have done. Their lack of enthusiasm remained a mystery to me for a long time, but one must allow for cultural differences in self-expression. What was uppermost to me was a job well done, a contented client and a well informed and entertained public.

We were invited back to create other segments for the "Dinah!" show, as we had certainly proved our creativity and professionalism with her and the producers, over and over again.

13

Snoopy For President

☆ ☆

Of all the celebrities we have had contact with, Charles Schultz's "Snoopy" is one of the most memorable to us. Our client, Weber's Bread, had a long-term contract to use Snoopy in its advertising programs. We publicized the idea of having the cute and popular cartoon pooch make an unofficial bid for the U.S. presidency in 1980, the year Ronald Reagan ran against Jimmy Carter. So Snoopy threw his hat—or should I say, his long, floppy ears—into the political ring.

A fantastic opportunity came up involving the big, annual "Ontario 500" auto race, which took place at the once-famous Ontario Motor Speedway in Ontario, California. The well-known racetrack is no longer there, having been torn down in the mid-1980s. The Ontario 500 was the nation's second largest auto racing event of the year. Only the Indianapolis 500 drew a larger crowd of spectators. All the major, highly-celebrated race drivers competed in the Ontario 500: Mario Andretti, Bobby Unser, Al Unser, A.J. Foyt, and many others. The event was televised nationally on "NBC Sports" and drew a wide viewing audience, while about 30,000 spectators crowded the stands.

Snoopy and "Miss Ontario Speedway" get together before the race.

☆ ☆

At the time, Howard was working with several radio stations in Los Angeles on various promotions for Weber's Bread. One of the stations was KLAC radio, the number one country music station. It also carried different sports broadcasts, including the Ontario 500 race. Always looking for on-air promotional opportunities to get extra exposure for our clients, Howard—half-jokingly—made a suggestion to the station's promotional manager. Since Weber's was the top-selling white bread in Southern California, and was also an advertiser on the station, why not find a way to use the product's popular mascot, Snoopy, at the race?

"What did you have in mind?" the promotional manager asked. "How about having Snoopy appear just before the race, since it is being promoted as a family event and everybody loves the famous cartoon dog," Howard replied.

"I suppose you'd like Snoopy to be the grand marshal of the pre-race parade, too?"

Howard naturally replied, "Why not? It would be a great gimmick. I can see it now—"Snoopy for President" leading the pre-race parade."

The promotional manager thought for a moment. "We were going to ask Buzz Aldrin to lead the parade. After all, he walked on the moon." (Buzz Aldrin was the second astronaut to walk on the moon after Neil Armstrong's historic first giant step for mankind in 1969.)

"Just think about it and let me know," Howard said. Surprisingly, he called Howard the next day and said, "Let's do it!"

That was the good news. The bad news was we had less than two weeks to coordinate everything. Snoopy was actually chosen to be the Grand Marshal for the event. Snoopy would lead a procession before the race began, driving one lap around the race course with all of the participating race drivers, and 15 local beauty queens following behind. Astronaut Buzz Aldrin was to be in the car directly behind Snoopy's. This was a big opportunity for Weber's Bread, as Snoopy's sponsor, and this was a major job for Lee & Associates.

We quickly lined up a young college woman from a temporary employment agency who lived in Upland, near the racetrack, to wear a Snoopy costume. Our big problem was finding a convertible to rent for the occasion; we had very little time to shop around for one. We called all of the new car dealers in town, requesting use of a convertible in exchange for the major publicity we had to offer. Either they didn't get back to us in time, or they didn't see the advantage of having one of their cars seen on television, as well as in newspapers, for positive national

☆ ☆

exposure. So we thought about renting a car. Hard to believe, but convertibles for rent in Southern California were not easy to come by. After calling every auto rental agency in town, we finally found one with a convertible available. To our chagrin, it was an ancient 1971 Cadillac; but as beggars, we didn't have time to be choosers. It looked beautiful and shiny, but the salesman at the rental agency gave us a word of caution, "It doesn't run as well as it looks." We were later to find out that was quite an understatement.

I'll relate how the day of the auto race went from the beginning, as my sons described it:

Howard picked up my other son, Frank, in the convertible around 6:45 a.m. on that fateful Sunday morning, about four hours prior to the Ontario 500 race. They had to pick up the young woman in Upland, who would don the Snoopy costume, and be at the racetrack by 10:30 a.m. They figured they had time for a coffee shop breakfast before the 45-minute drive from Los Angeles to Upland and over to the racetrack at nearby Ontario. They thought they'd have PLENTY of time to spare.

One thing they did not anticipate was having any problems with the car! I guess you could say they had a warning of things to come, though. As soon as Frank got into the car and was about to close the passenger door, the handle came off in his hand! They couldn't get it back on, because it wouldn't snap in properly. On top of this omen of unpleasant things to come, the weather was quite chilly. Being early in the morning, it was very cold outside, and they were going to be driving (presumably rather fast) on the freeway, so they wanted to put the car roof up. They struggled and wrestled with it, but they just couldn't close it all the way. The lever on the passenger-side latch of the canvas top just would not fit! Frank, as the passenger, began to imagine that this car had it in for him personally. They kept trying to force it to close, with no luck whatsoever. Howard and Frank must have been in a Charlie Chaplin comedy in a past life. That's what it felt like to them: Charlie Chaplin in one of his early short comedy films, trying to ready the vehicle for a Sunday drive and everything goes askew. They finally got the top partially closed, but couldn't secure it all the way. They felt it was good enough for now, since it would only be for the short drive to the racetrack. Short drive, yes, but they didn't know how L-O-N-G that drive was about to take.

So they took time for a nice, big breakfast to last them throughout what was sure to be a very busy day. Then they were on their way. It was only around 7:45 a.m. or so; they still had plenty of time. Famous

☆ ☆

last words, right? When they got on the freeway and accelerated into the fast lane, Frank and Howard noticed a huge white cloud of smoke in their rear-view mirror. At first, they wondered what kind of moron would drive such a vehicle on the freeway. Then Howard realized it was coming out of their old Caddie convertible's exhaust pipe! He said he felt as if they were in James Bond, Agent 007's car, releasing a smoke screen on any bad guys following behind them! Frank said the auto rental agency must not have changed the oil in this car for 10 years!

They began to panic because here they were about to lead a parade around the Ontario Speedway racetrack in front of 30,000 people and a nationally televised audience, and nobody would be able to see the celebrity race drivers behind them because of all the smoke! WHAT A TOTAL NIGHTMARE!!!

Worse yet, they were in immediate danger of creating a traffic jam—or, heaven forbid—an accident on the freeway. It wouldn't take long for the California Highway Patrol (a.k.a. "CHiPs" to avid '80s television viewers) to spot them. They slowed down, and noticed that the smoke didn't come out if they drove under 30 miles-per-hour. They knew they wouldn't be driving over 5 miles-per-hour during the parade, anyhow, so they could safely control the car's smoke problem. So much for "life in the fast lane." They chugged across four lanes of traffic to the far right, slow lane. At least they'd be safe there, if they weren't pulled over by the highway patrol for going under the legal minimum speed limit.

Not wanting to take any chances, they drove all the way to Ontario, carefully going only 30-mph on the freeway, with cars constantly honking and passing them, as if they didn't realize they had a problem!

They became even more alarmed about the suspect convertible when they realized that it would take them twice as long to get to the speedway, and they still had to pick up "Ms. Snoopy" in Upland. They could only hope they'd still be able to make it there with some time to spare.

They later told me that driving that slowly on a near-empty freeway seemed to take forever! It felt like being trapped inside a slow motion movie. But any time the speedometer climbed above 30 mph, the smoke came back! It was almost like the reverse of the Sandra Bullock movie "Speed," featuring a bus rigged to explode if it's driven slower than 50 mph. It is rather ironic that they were on their way to a major auto race, isn't it?

The situation seemed to be going rather smoothly—all things consid-

☆ ☆ ☆ ☆ ☆ ☆ ☆ ☆ ☆ ☆ ☆ ☆ ☆ ☆ ☆ ☆ ☆ ☆ ☆ ☆

ered—until they got about five miles before their exit in Upland to pick up the person who was to wear the Snoopy costume. They were driving along, when all of a sudden there's a loud noise! Whump! The rooftop latch came apart, and the car roof flew up! Howard was ready to slow down, but saw a huge truck barreling up behind them. Meanwhile, Frank grabbed the roof, trying to hold it down himself, while they were driving down the freeway! They had to travel like this until they got to the off ramp! The truck kept honking for Howard to drive faster, eventually giving up and going around the puttering convertible.

Even at the snail's pace of 30-mph, it wasn't easy driving along like this. Frank said it really hurt his hand and arm while wrestling with that bouncing roof and trying to hold it in place. The strong wind resistance kept lifting it back up! Howard joined Frank in holding down the rooftop by using his left hand while keeping his right hand tightly on the steering wheel. Imagine trying to hold onto your hat on a blustery day, and multiply that experience about 100 times! The top was all the more difficult to maneuver because the two of them were laughing hysterically, and remember, it was cold outside. As in Snoopy's famous cartoon strip, they could just imagine the cute dog in the back seat with his portable typewriter, still trying to write the "world's greatest novel." Only this time it would begin, "It was a dark and chilly morning when something happened on the way to the racetrack...." Why Howard and Frank hadn't been spotted by the highway patrol or a traffic helicopter by now is one of the great mysteries of life.

As they finally approached the freeway exit in Upland, they thought their troubles were over. However, when they stopped at the red light at the end of the exit off-ramp, a lot of steam started gushing out from under the hood! The car was overheating! By the time the light turned green, the car had died! At least it waited until after they got off the freeway to give up the ghost. They couldn't get it started again! They just couldn't believe what was happening! They were hoping to awake from this terrible, surreal dream at any minute, but they weren't so lucky!

Howard and Frank had to push the car to a nearby gas station. It was a miracle that one was literally just around the corner, only about 25 yards away. Luck was finally with them—bad luck—because early on a Sunday morning, no garage mechanic was on duty there!

It was now almost 9:30 a.m. They had to be at the racetrack and ready to go in little more than an hour, and they were still about 25 minutes away. So while they let the car cool off from its "exhausting" 30-mph freeway adventure, they called "Ms. Snoopy" and asked her to meet them at the gas station. Expecting to have been picked up at her home 45 minutes earlier, the Snoopy girl said it would take her at least 20 minutes to get to them, since she had to find someone to give her a ride or else she would have to take a cab. (Don't forget, cell phones didn't exist back then, so they couldn't call her until they got off the freeway and found a pay phone.) Meanwhile, Howard and Frank again began having more panic attacks waiting for the engine to cool. After about 20 minutes or so, they put water in the radiator, and tried to start the car again; it wouldn't start! They were fast becoming total wrecks—just like the car! They kept thinking how embarrassing and humiliating it would be to have to cancel! Most of us would rather feel anything than humiliation, especially before a live television audience of millions. How could they lead a nationally televised parade for an auto race with a car that didn't work?

Well, by the time "Ms. Snoopy" arrived, it was just after 10 a.m. Suddenly, they were pushing a vital deadline, though they had started out earlier at a well-organized, leisurely pace. This was getting a little too suspenseful. Seasoned public relations counselors like Howard and Frank are normally used to dealing with crises; it goes with the territory of what they do. "Never say die," as the old saying goes. They tried to start the car once again, and when they turned the ignition, it started! Whew, what a relief!

They proceeded to the racetrack, going faster than the 30-mph they had been traveling (who cared about white smoke at this point?). Talk about making a grand entrance. By the time they arrived and checked in for their press credentials, it was just moments before the procession was set to begin. Parade officials rushed them onto the racetrack, and quickly positioned them in the lead.

Part of the Snoopy (and Weber's Bread) pre-race promotion.

☆ ☆

Howard was driving the car, Snoopy sat poised on top of the back seat —waving and blowing kisses to the crowd—and Frank was at the inside edge of the racetrack, ready to start taking publicity pictures. (Thank goodness I wasn't the one driving!) Howard cupped his hands around his mouth, so he could yell to Frank over the noise of the crowd, and told him the car was idling even worse.

He felt sure the car was going to die on him while leading the parade. They were so emotionally strung out by this time, they didn't know whether to laugh, cry or have a heart attack! They held their breath as the parade director gave Howard the "go" signal, and he proceeded very slowly to lead the motorcade one lap around the racetrack. Grand Marshal Snoopy, wearing a sewed-on costume grin, continued waving to the crowd; the show must go on despite transportation problems. What a trouper, Snoopy!

The NBC cameras were focused right on the car, and Howard was screaming with laughter inside his head as he gave Frank a thumbs-up, while at the same time praying the car could make just one lap around the track. Meanwhile, Frank was snapping away, making sure to capture the moment on film. A big white banner on each side of the blue Cadillac proclaimed in giant letters, "Weber's Bread Supports Snoopy for Presi-

Snoopy greets 30,000 race fans, while
Howard drives and prays the old Caddie doesn't die during the pre-race parade.

dent." After all, this is why they were at the event in the first place, for publicity! These photos would be sent to newspapers for extra exposure for Weber's bread.

Howard later said, to be honest, he couldn't remember how long it took to drive the one lap around the track, but it seemed like an eternity! He somehow, some way, made it, without the car dying, without the car overheating, and without any white smoke coming out of the exhaust. It really was a miracle. In the back of his mind, Howard thought about how Buzz Aldrin—who had actually walked on the moon and was acknowledged as one of the greatest heroes on earth—was in the second car behind Snoopy. He felt a little guilty about getting the lead over this famous astronaut, and would have felt even worse if the convertible had started oozing smoke again, right in his face!.

As Howard was driving the car to the parking zone, Frank caught up to them and hopped into the front seat, and believe it or not, the car died. They had to push it several yards into the parking area, fortunately out of range of the NBC cameras! They were still in shock, but so very relieved that they had pulled off the event without embarrassing themselves, Weber's bread, and the Ontario 500 racing committee.

After the procession and just before the race, Howard arranged for one of KLAC Radio's sports reporters to "interview" Snoopy live on-air. The famous pooch held a loaf of Weber's bread, as a visual, while posing with the reporter for photos which were shot by Frank and about two dozen media photographers. This helped garner lots of publicity for Weber's bread, in addition to the television exposure we had just received during the pre-race lap. As for the interview, since Snoopy (as a cartoon character) doesn't actually talk, the reporter did a brief tongue-in-cheek interview with Howard, Snoopy's personal driver and confidant. The reporter described to the listeners how he was standing with Snoopy, just yards away from the world's top race car drivers and their super-fast cars. Radio listeners could hear the noise of the engines revving up and the loud background roar of 30,000 racing fans yelling from the bleachers. Howard told the reporter how much Snoopy appreciated having Weber's Bread support him for the U.S. Presidency, and what a thrill it was to be the Grand Marshal of the last official Ontario 500 race. Also, it was very exciting for Snoopy to personally meet Buzz Aldrin, because he walked on the moon!

At the end of the long day, Howard, Frank, and "Ms. Snoopy" sat quietly in the Caddie during the late afternoon dusk. Exhausted from all

☆ ☆ ☆ ☆ ☆ ☆ ☆ ☆ ☆ ☆ ☆ ☆ ☆ ☆ ☆ ☆ ☆ ☆ ☆ ☆

the hoopla, they were finally out of the limelight, resting and making sure the unreliable engine was cool once more, before venturing on their leisurely drive home, thankfully without any deadline restraints. After they got going, they dropped off "Ms. Snoopy," then drove for at least 15 minutes without saying anything to each other, totally drained by their experience. While traveling their self-imposed slow speed limit, they hit a small bump in the slow lane and the glove-box door popped off—PA—CHUNG!—and landed in Frank's lap! They looked at each other in amazement, for just a moment, then burst out with the chuckles. They started laughing so hard, tears came streaming out of their eyes. Howard yelled "Screw it," hit the gas pedal, and cranked the old Caddie up to the legal limit of 65-mph. They guffawed all the way home, the car sputtering and spewing a trail of white smoke up behind them. It was like the happy ending of a Charlie Chaplin movie as they sped off into the sunset, heads shaking with laughter.

14

Foiled By Fate

☆ ☆

In 1949, Capt. Ed Murphy, a development engineer at Edwards Air Force Base in Muroc, California, became frustrated with a project, due to a wiring error made by a technician. He was heard to remark, "If there is any way to do it wrong, he will," referring to the technician who had apparently caused the wiring glitch. His statement became known as "Murphy's Law," and the rest is history. We have all heard Murphy's maxim jokingly used for many years in America's workplaces: "If anything can go wrong, it will."

In the public relations business, Murphy's Law can reach crisis proportions, even against astronomical odds. Two such big, unexpected occurrences affected us very much. Just before Thanksgiving in 1963, we were doing a television blitz to promote turkeys and Mrs. Cubbison's Dressing (a ready-made, turkey dressing mix). We scheduled cooking demonstrations on practically every TV station in Los Angeles. In those days, many food programs were on the air, on every network, often scheduled between a movie and a talk show. This was before the days of cable TV, when no public television "cooking shows" or The Food Network existed.

We spent weeks putting the promotional campaign together. We studied the minute details of creating a complete Thanksgiving Day food table and display, with enough food for the entire crews of each show. We instructed our spokespersons—who were home economists, chefs, and actresses—to say positive words about turkey and stuffing, and to remind viewers of the following catch phrase: "Why wait until Thanksgiving? Anytime is Turkey Time."

We had already done one early morning TV show on Friday, November 22, 1963, and were working on another show that same morning. In the middle of our next demonstration, a seemingly impossible news item broke around the world: "United States President John Fitzgerald Kennedy had been fatally shot." What a shocker! Of course, our two other food demonstrations scheduled for that day at other stations had to be scrapped. The world came to a stop. We were all sick to our stomachs at the horrifying news of our President being gunned down in the streets, in a so-called civilized society. It was the worst possible time to do any Thanksgiving promotion at all. To tell you the truth, hardly anyone wanted to eat the delectable food feasts we had prepared for the shows, so we left it packed up for the studio crews to take home with them. The nation was in terrible shock, a state that lasted for several days. Even decades later, Americans are still affected by that tragedy. Of course, our meticulously planned Thanksgiving food shows went the way of all leftovers.

It got worse from there. Every year, the National Turkey Federation would send a turkey to the White House. The President would donate the turkey to a local petting zoo; the famous bird was thus given a stay of execution. In that ill-fated Thanksgiving year, we represented the California Turkey Advisory Board and suggested they send the President the new "white feathered turkey." Bob McPherrin, our client, was chairman of the Turkey Board. It was Bob's father who had bred this unusual, broad-breasted, snow white bird.

We arranged to send the uniquely-bred turkey to the White House for the annual Thanksgiving photo to be taken with the President, one that would be sent out for publicity purposes to help us get additional positive exposure in the media. We suggested the turkey be standing in a shallow cardboard box with a sign reading, "Good eating, Mr. President," as

President Kennedy being presented
with his special Thanksgiving turkey that fateful year, 1963.

☆ ☆

we thought that this extra little message would help us get more media coverage. The photo, which had been taken several days in advance of Thanksgiving, featured President Kennedy, Senator Everett Dirkson, our client Bob McPherrin and other leaders in the turkey industry. I was all set to release my photos in California and to the grocery trade press nationally, when this tragic event in American history occurred, the appalling assassination of President Kennedy. The untimely photos never went out the door, and were kept for decades in a box in our office. We eventually lost track of them. In recent years, Time magazine, which had one of the few remaining copies of that same photo, ran it on the cover, along with similar Thanksgiving photos of other presidents, taken over the years.

☆ ☆ ☆

One of our biggest crises, which also coincidentally relates to Thanksgiving, occurred on November 10, 1959, which we have ever since referred to as "Black Cranberry Day." Pesticide used on the cranberry crop had apparently caused such a tremendous problem that the newspapers were full of headlines. In recent years, we've had food scares with the apple crop and with contaminated grapes from Chile. But those were minor flare-ups compared to the big cranberry scare of '59. We did not work for the cranberry growers at that time, but they were friends of ours. We had many promotional tie-ins together and occasionally we had assignments from them. So, suddenly we were involved. The cranberry scare was like the aftermath of one of our California earthquakes; the shock waves just kept on rolling, and the repercussions affected us too, because of our involvement with the California Turkey Advisory Board. It practically wiped out the cranberry growers that year and also created sales problems for the turkey growers.

Adhering to Murphy's Law, the cranberry scare occurred just before Thanksgiving, our national day of feasting. In fact, the centuries-old holiday highlights the tart berry; it is the only time of the year when cans of cranberry sauce are usually depleted from grocers' shelves. What is Thanksgiving without turkey and cranberry sauce to go with it? The headlines revved up on November 10, and continued through our traditional "Day of Thanks" before the hoopla died down. Cranberries disappeared from grocers' shelves for all the wrong reasons.

Influential leaders in our society were jumping on the cranberry-scare bandwagon: the Secretary of Heath, Education and Welfare; the Secretary of Agriculture; the Food and Drug Administration (FDA); and

☆ ☆

government departments in all the states that produced cranberries. You would have thought it was about to be an election issue. Even U.S. President Dwight Eisenhower commented at the time, "The Secretary warns that some Washington and Oregon crops are contaminated with the weed-killer aminotriazole, which induces cancer in rats." That comment became just one of many frightening headlines, blazing across the New York Times, no less. A major news conference was held to advise the public against buying cranberries if their source was not known. As a result of this commotion, cranberries were whisked off the shelves, restaurants scratched them off their menu, and homemakers had to pore over recipe books at the last minute to find substitute sauces to serve with their holiday birds.

Almost every government agency came out of the woodwork and got involved, many of which the public had never heard of before the cranberry scare reared its ugly head. The FDA ordered practically its entire field staff to make a nationwide check for contaminated cranberries.

To calm the public furor down, the U.S. Secretary of Agriculture, Ezra Taft Benson, said that he would eat cranberries on Thanksgiving Day. And Vice President Richard Nixon said that his family would eat cranberries with turkey for the holiday. Senators and governors from the five states that grew cranberries sent wires to Washington, D.C. demanding President Eisenhower call for a probe into the matter and get cranberries back on the dinner table.

In short, all hell broke loose over a little berry that was otherwise poised and ready for its holiday revue. The horror for us is that we knew the cranberry scare would affect turkey sales, too. We got as busy as a beehive, trying to obtain as much good news about the positive tests on cranberries as we could possibly gather. Then we sent the information to the newspapers, radio and TV stations. As in all crises of this sort, our research showed that only a limited amount of cranberries were found with the particular contaminates. Soon, grocery markets put labels on the non-contaminated cans marking them as safe. The cranberry growers did a great deal of testing and spent a lot of money trying to undo the hysteria, and even though Thanksgiving was a bust that year, by the time Christmas rolled around, things were almost back to normal. During those four weeks between Thanksgiving and Christmas, we avoided the negative and accentuated the positive aspects of turkey and its cranberry accompaniment.

In the new millennium, cranberries are "in" now. Ironically, the

☆ ☆

Jamba Juice chain offers a favorite juice smoothie called "Cranberry Craze." So we've gone from being cranberry scared to cranberry crazed. I guess all that positive publicity caught on over the decades.

☆ ☆ ☆

When it came to promoting turkeys, it seemed inevitable that practically every year one major event or gathering, with a large number of people, would result in a headline such as "Food Poisoning at Turkey Dinner." Here again, we had to stop everything and contact the board of health to determine the real story. Nine times out of ten, the real problem was the sauce, the mayonnaise or a sick food handler, and not the turkey or the stuffing itself. Over and over, we tried our best to educate people on how to cook a turkey dinner safely and how to protect themselves from improper food handling.

When a crisis comes, it is usually at the wrong time; that's one reason it is called a crisis. There is never a good time for anything to go wrong, but an ill-fated occurrence—on top of poor timing—is disastrous. You've got to stop what you are doing, immediately, and get on the crisis. It is especially bad when you are in the midst of another promotion, involved with another client's project, or on a vital deadline. It becomes an even scarier problem if key people are out of town, or the crisis erupts first thing in the morning (usually Monday), or the last thing of the day (usually Friday). Murphy's Law, I feel sure, has decreed Mondays and Fridays for fatalities to drop out of a black hole and land in the middle of one's best laid plans.

One thing for sure, in a major crisis, everything comes to a stop, and all of our office action and energy shifts immediately to the crisis. The perfect study of this subject is what I call "The Frito-Lay Incident," which occurred in 1977. Lee & Associates was handling public relations on the West Coast for Frito-Lay, makers of Fritos, the popular corn chips, and other snack products. Late one afternoon, a consumer reporter on KCBS, our local CBS affiliate here in Los Angeles, went into the studio commissary and bought a bag of Fritos corn chips out of a vending machine. When she opened the bag, she discovered a few extra chips had been added—metal chips; that is, a few tiny bits of metal were in the bag. Murphy's Law had timed this occurrence just before the six-o'clock news, of course. The reporter took the bag with her onto the news set. When it came time for her segment to air, she said something akin to the following: "I'm not going to give my regular report tonight, because something just happened to me at the snack machine." She then held up the suspect bag of Fritos for the camera—and all of Southern California—to see. "Frito-Lay apparently has a new kind of chip product on the market—metal chips!" As you can imagine, it went downhill from there.

The news spread like wildfire through the Frito-Lay company, word-of-mouth being the fleetest of messengers. Within hours, it got to the Vice President of Public Relations at the Frito-Lay headquarters in Dallas, Texas, who was both a client and a friend of mine. The next morning, the Vice President of Quality Control flew out to Los Angeles to help us sort out the situation. We met at the local Frito-Lay plant to find out how the metal had gotten into the bag of chips. I knew the plant manager well, and discovered he had already investigated the problem. The plant had regular inspections and all equipment was kept running efficiently. Unfortunately, a small mechanical failure had occurred between inspections, a situation that was not readily detectable. A piece of a conveyor belt had worn out, and little bits of metal had chipped off in the process and landed in a few of the bags. The efficient plant manager was able to determine, by the coding on the bags, exactly where the suspect chips had gone out to the public. Fortunately, they had only been placed in selected vending machines, in the Hollywood area, and had not been stocked in supermarkets. The mutant bags of Fritos corn chips were quickly apprehended by Frito-Lay personnel, and no further incidents of metal were reported.

I quickly called the consumer reporter at KCBS, and invited her to bring a camera crew down to the Frito-Lay plant. We wanted to show them, step by step, how the chips are made, and have the camera crew tape the process. We showed the consumer reporter where the mechanical breakdown had occurred and what steps had been taken to quickly remedy the problem. On that evening's newscast, she lauded the Frito-Lay company for jumping on a potential problem and solving it so quickly. She showed footage of how the tasty corn chips were made, as well as the high degree of quality control the company uses. In effect, her broadcast was an unexpected, positive commercial for Frito-Lay. So, you see, not all problems are what they appear to be. The reporter had fortunately called attention to a serious situation that could have reached disastrous proportions, had any of the metal bits been ingested by unsuspecting consumers. By acting on the situation immediately, the image of the Frito-Lay company was actually enhanced in the public's mind. To me, this is one of the most prime examples of turning an emergency situation into an asset.

☆ ☆

One of our earliest clients was LASCCO, the Los Angeles Smoking and Curing Company, which is one of the largest producers of smoked and pickled fish in the United States. Their products include smoked salmon, smoked whitefish, herring, caviar, and cod. I knew LASCCO owner Louis Vitale as a fine gentleman who was totally immersed in the business he had run since 1920. He was dedicated to producing the very best product. In addition, he was quite a philanthropist, and everyone liked Louis. But Louis' business was about to be affected in the worst way by Murphy's Law.

As I recall, during one year, an entire family in Tennessee got botulism from eating smoked whitefish and died. Even then, without the instant communication that we have available to us now, the whole world knew about it immediately. The U.S. government, in its haste and panic, condemned all smoked whitefish as soon as the botulism story broke, with no regard to where the tainted whitefish had actually originated. In Los Angeles, all the whitefish was instantly recalled and my friend Louis was devastated. That particular story occupied the news media for quite a while and practically wiped out the whitefish business.

To show you how impersonal Murphy's Law can be, LASCCO was getting its fish from an area that was not contaminated; the LASCCO products had never had any incident of contamination. The government came up with blanket rules and regulations to have the smokers cook the whitefish at a higher degree of heat to kill bacteria. Louis complied, and little by little, like any other crisis, it wore off and things got back to normal, even though he had never been the culprit in the first place.

But the trouble didn't end there. The media quite often come back around on an anniversary to update a story from previous years. For some reason that I could never understand—because the story certainly didn't warrant it—a year later, the Saturday Evening Post came out with a big feature article about the tainted fish. The gist of the story was: "It has been a year since the whitefish scare, let's see what's happening." Suddenly the media brought more attention to an old subject without any regard to the problems that fish marketers would face from a selling point of view. The consumers were scared to death by the reminder all over again, which was an unnecessary promotion of fear. After a year of building the whitefish business back up again, it was thrown into a depressed situation once more.

Louis Vitale was again distraught because he was so proud of his products. As any small-business person knows, pride is a strong motivator for being in business for oneself. His immediate reaction was typical of most clients on hearing of "bad press" for no good reason; Louis called me and said he wanted to sue the Saturday Evening Post for ruining his business. "Contact them and tell them to make a retraction," he said. "Make them realize all the trouble they have caused for my business."

But we knew that game plan just wouldn't work. "Louis, we know we can get more by using honey, rather than vinegar," I told him. "Let me contact the Saturday Evening Post directly, in person, and see what we can do."

While I was in New York on behalf of another client, I visited the Saturday Evening Post editorial offices. I managed to meet both the editor and the reporter who had written the updated scare story on smoked whitefish. I pointed out what a horrible thing they had done inadvertently to the whitefish industry, in general, by focusing on one occurrence of contamination. What good did they do by calling up the story a year after the fact? The contamination problem had been solved, no one else had gotten sick, and this recap story would only have a strong negative effect on consumer confidence. Is there any way they could help out the smoked fish industry?

After much discussion, the Saturday Evening Post editor remembered that the staff was in the midst of doing a summer barbecue story, featuring California and several famous people. At last Murphy's Law was working in reverse! I discussed my credentials with the Post staff and told them I could get them more celebrities. Even better, I could supply a home economist to help out with appropriate recipes. After all, California is the home of barbecues. I told them I would submit recipes for the article, ones that would include the use of smoked fish in the generic sense; whitefish would not be specifically mentioned. Let's face it, smoked fish by itself really isn't very exciting and I didn't want the story to flounder. Obviously, smoked fish would have to be part of an overall, glamorous barbecue menu.

They agreed with this proposal and said we had to work quickly as they had already begun planning the issue and were on a tight schedule. Celebrities such as Tippi Hedren of Alfred Hitchcock's "The Birds," who is well known to a later generation as the mother of popular actress Melanie Griffith, was already set to attend. We were also able to get Steve Allen who was a terrific guest. The most challenging item on our list of ideas was to get the current governor of California to participate; it would be ideal if Governor Edmund G. Brown Sr. could have a typical California barbecue. However, a barbecue of this magnitude would be a very time-consuming event. Even with careful planning, the personnel involved have to take time away from their busy schedules. The first thing to do was to get the governor's permission. Although we had an opportunity to promote California fish products favorably, frankly, we did not think that was strong enough to entice the governor's participation. So we decided to go through the California director of agriculture to get to the governor's office. We would attempt to have him convince the governor that we had an opportunity to promote California commodities, very positively and (literally!) in good taste. Here was an opportunity to show how important California's agriculture and fishing industry were to the state's economy. We then contacted the governor's wife, a very gracious lady, and asked her if we could impose upon her to use the backyard of the governor's mansion for a summer barbecue. We also wanted to design a menu based on what she might serve at a barbecue for her family or friends.

To our delight, the governor's office okayed our proposal. We had our home economist travel to the state capitol in Sacramento to meet with Mrs. Brown and discuss how she cooked a turkey. (By this time, we also brought in the California Turkey Advisory Board to participate in

California Governor Edmund G. (Pat) Brown carving a barbecued turkey in the 1970s.

the barbecue. It was an open door opportunity for many of our clients and their related industries.) We asked her permission to use particular foods, if they would indeed fit into her menu. Thus, we built the whole barbecue around California turkeys, including smoked seafood, and ended up with quite an event we might never have thought of without the intervention of Murphy's Law in the first place.

The Saturday Evening Post photo team, their editorial team, and our team all showed up and spent a very long day at the governor's mansion. Hundreds of photos were taken and we managed to provide tested recipes that were acceptable to the Brown family.

It's interesting to note that later on, their son, Jerry Brown would follow in his father's footsteps to become California's governor in the 1980s, and their daughter, Kathleen Brown, became California's state treasurer. At the time of our barbecue, they were both youngsters.

Everyone was happy, and incidentally, we accomplished a positive image for smoked and pickled fish that were presented as part of the barbecue menu. Sometimes it pays to flaunt Murphy's Law right in the face with energetic action; what started out as an attempt to thwart the effects of negative publicity turned into a gala event that made a lot of people happy and informed the nation about California's fine products.

Murphy's Law only stays dormant for so long. Crises pop up on a regular basis. Sometimes you pray your product is not the one the Center for Science in the Public Interest and the politicians in Washington hit on. Food scares of late include theater popcorn, Mexican food, Chinese food, chicken, beef, strawberries and even orange juice. The headlines hit hard, and instantly the radio and TV news crews pick it up and then the talk shows, spinning it through a complete media cycle.

We had that continuous cycle with seafood when we were representing the California Fisheries and Seafood Institute. We were thrown into an endless barrage of bad news, while simultaneously, we distributed a steady stream of good news to the media about the healthful qualities of fish. We were given favorable themes by the National Fisheries Institute and the National Seafood Council to use in our publicity. We had nutritionists telling the public things like: "Eat fish three times a week," "Eat fish, live better," "Omega three fatty acids are great for health," and "Fish is low in fat and easy to digest." The many good, healthful qualities of fish were perpetually promoted. Then came the bad news! Murphy's Law was lurking not too far away. Many times exaggerated and many times out of context, issues flared up about fish having a high mercury content, fish comes from polluted waters, contaminated oysters can kill you, and on and on.

The biggest problem we ran into was dealing with the constituents—the fishermen, the processors, the distributors, the retailers—who railed at us: "What are you doing about this? Stop all of the bad news! Call the newspapers! Call the TV! Tell them they are wrong!" It got so that the reaction from within the industry was much harder to deal with than the reaction from the consumers. We spent a lot of our time responding instantly, "putting out fires"—drop everything that you're doing and deal with the crisis issue at hand—right NOW. Often, against our clients' wishes, we opted to not do anything and let the monster lie still. Our theory was that, if we stirred up the negative publicity, we would only remind the public of it and, unfortunately, inform other people for the first time. It would be better to let the issue blow over than give the media a rebuttal. Besides, within a week or two, another crisis would crop up about some other product, and the media would then beat that one to to death, diverting their attention.

At all times, we presented the positive information we had on fish and seafood. We constantly generated news releases and feature stories. We created videos, interviews and cooking demonstrations, pointing out the tremendously healthful qualities of fish and seafood. We quoted a wide variety of authorities, including scientists, doctors, nutritionists, cookbook authors, and dietitians. We called upon the key officers and directors of seafood plants in Los Angeles to show the media that they had an efficient and clean processing operation. We showed the retailers the efficiencies of sanitary handling. Naturally, we told the consumers to use good common sense and buy from reliable retailers.

One big victory for us occurred when the Los Angeles Times printed a story misquoting the FDA by saying that the consumer had a whopping 20% chance of eating contaminated seafood. We singled out several such statements from the powerful newspaper condemning seafood as very bad, contaminated food. We, and our related food associations, contacted the FDA and were able to get a proper response. For the first time that we knew of, we were able to get the FDA to send out a news release responding to that particular story, calling it "inaccurate, misleading and misrepresenting preliminary results of one of its surveys."

Maintaining the pressure, we used the power of letters-to-the-editor. I wrote a letter to the editor on behalf of the president of the California Fisheries and Seafood Institute responding to the article; it specifically included the proper statistics and the news that the FDA also responded to the inaccurate, negative article. The letter was printed in the Los Angeles Times about a week later. Several other newspapers, as well as the electronic media, picked up the story from the FDA. This is what I call a victory; it solved the problem for our nervous constituents from the seafood industry. Responsible public relations goes beyond educating the public. We enlisted the aid of one of our consultants, Dr. Bob Price, a scientist at the University of California at Davis, to present facts, figures and guidelines for the proper handling of fish and seafood. We put this information in a booklet form and distributed it to every major seafood handler in California, covering every known issue.

To illustrate how random Murphy's Law is, "The great Florida 2000 Presidential Vote Count Broo-Ha-Ha" (Al Gore vs. George W. Bush) began during our busiest time for our client, Mrs. Cubbison's Dressing Mix. (Approaching Thanksgiving and Christmas is when most of Mrs. Cubbison's sales are made.) All of our planned radio and TV publicity takes place at this time. We scheduled several spokespeople, including myself, to be interviewed in the media, and all we got were cancellations and segment time reductions because they were "waiting for the latest news"—for days! Not a good way for any client to start their biggest time of the year. Fortunately, through persistence, we managed to get a good number of radio interviews and TV cooking demonstrations, helping our client meet their expected sales goals.

Murphy's Law may seem like a killer, but if you grab it by the throat, you can use its doom-like nature to turn seemingly disastrous events into major triumphs, as in the Frito-Lay incident. I personally feel many of our successes in life are spurred by the creative energy that can evolve from a crisis.

15

The Wild Honey Caper

☆ ☆

Back in the days when there were more newspapers around, a photo in the (now defunct) Los Angeles Herald Express really caught my eye. For a moment, I thought I had a "copycat" promoter at large, because the photo and accompanying caption were much like something I would generate. The picture featured a very attractive young lady and the caption read, "Wild About Wild Honey. Hollywood wolves, among others, will be salivating about Miss Wild Honey, Marguerite Barbera of Hollywood, as much as a bear, should he run into a wild honey tree in the woods...."

We were getting ready to publicize "National Honey Week," in the early 1950s, to promote our client, Superior Honey. At first, I thought someone was stealing our thunder and had the jump on promoting honey. It turned out to be simply a publicity stunt by Capitol Records for a record called "Wild Honey" by a new singer named John Arsesi. (I later found out that John Arsesi was being promoted very aggressively by a group trying to put him on the map, in a manner similar to Frank

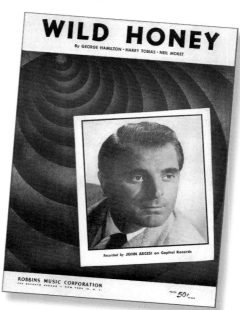

Singer John Arsesi's "Wild Honey" started the whole promotion and commotion.

Sinatra's promotion in the early 1940s.)

Whew—not only did I not have a rival honey promoter out there, but here was a giant opportunity to do a tie-in with the record's promotion. You could even say it was a honey of a deal.

I contacted the publicity director at Capitol Records, Bud Freeman. "Mr. Freeman, Lee & Associates represents the largest honey company in the United States, and we are preparing to promote honey for National Honey Week, and why don't we get together?" I pitched to him, thinking I was going to get involved in an ordinary tie-in promotion that would be mutually beneficial.

Well, that one phone call turned into "Wild Honey" all right. In fact, it turned out to be a little wilder than we ever expected. We went from the conservative food industry point-of-view to the wild record industry point-of-view. It was like switching from a leisurely drive in the country to a major auto race; things happened much faster than we anticipated.

We agreed to provide Capitol Records with honey products and publicity support with generic background information on honey and all its good qualities. Our honeyed conversation went something like this:

"We absolutely must have our Miss Wild Honey as the spokesperson," Freeman said. "Capitol Records insists on it."

I countered by saying, "We should have several 'honeys,' so that Miss Wild Honey can stand out." That's how Miss Superior

Honey and Record Promotion

Spencer Redfield, sales manager of Superior Honey Co., surrounded by a group of Superior Honeys at the recent Honey-and-Feather party in honor of National Honey Week.

Superior Honey Co. recently tied in with Capitol Records and John Arcesi during National Honey Week to promote honey and the Capitol record, "Wild Honey."

Leo Pearlstein, president of Lee & Associates, handled all the details for this very successful promotion.

It all started with a picture of "Miss Wild Honey" in the newspapers. Upon investigation, Mr. Pearlstein discovered that Capitol Records was embarking upon a publicity campaign to promote Johnnie Arcesi, one of their new singers, and his record, "Wild Honey."

The publicity men of the respective organizations decided to use the impetus of National Honey Week to jointly promote Superior Honey and Capitol Records.

One hundred leading disc jockeys, editors, etc., received personal invitations to a honey-and-feather party, at which event John Arcesi was to crown Miss Superior Honey, to be chosen from a bevy of Hollywood's most beautiful honeys: Miss Jellied Honey, Miss Honey Butter, Miss Sage Honey, Miss Clover Honey, Miss Creamed Honey, Miss Comb Honey, etc.

The newsreels and columnists turned out en masse, releasing a multitude of news releases pertaining to this event and National Honey Week.

The TV newsreels and news rooms broadcast this news as well.

The grocery trade was informed of the promotion so that they could tie in and take full advantage.

Grocery trade feature letting the industry know about the honey promotion.

☆ ☆

Honey, Miss Honey-and-Butter, Miss Jellied Honey, and Miss Clover Honey all came to bee—er—be, that is.

In the '50s, the Garden of Allah Hotel in Hollywood, was an "in spot." So Capitol Records decided to have a "honey and feather" party there. They would invite all the local newspaper reporters, the radio disc jockeys (after all, they wanted to promote the record), the news-wire services, movie newsreel cameramen and news reporters from the still quite young TV industry. We also invited the supermarket executives and trade magazine reporters.

In making the invitations, we obtained feathers from the Southern California Poultry Company, another one of our clients, put them in little plastic bags and then into a box with a small jar of Superior Honey. The invitations were sent out by us and Capitol Records, each using different approaches, tying everything into National Honey Week. We had Capitol Records send personal letters to the retailers and the deejays, signed by Miss Wild Honey, who invited them to participate in the honey-and-feather event. We planned to have a drawing, and the winner would get to personally "pick the feathers off" Miss Wild Honey.

John Arsesi poses with "Miss Wild Honey" (Marguerite Barbera) and his recording of "Wild Honey."

☆ ☆

NATIONAL HONEY WEEK

National Honey Week will be observed October 26-November 2. The United States Department of Agriculture, Production and Market Administration is cooperating with the American Beekeeping Federation in this observance. This year, a quarter billion pounds of honey will be produced in United States. Vigorous promotion of the abundant supply will mean increased sales for the retail grocer.

The B-Z-B Honey Company, Alhambra, California, is publicizing its 100% pure NATURAL honey by television, radio and store displays during the entire season.

Packer representation for the company is the L. W. Casey Co. (TRinity 5601). A phone call will bring a salesman and display material to any retail grocer in Southern California.

The front cover illustration is that of Mrs. H. H. Schumacher, attractive wife of Hans Schumacher, owner of B-Z-B Honey Company.

A National Honey Week announcement (placed in trade publications).

We were looking for maximum publicity, to impress both the retailers and the consumers about honey. The honey-and-feather idea, which came from the record promoters, was wild; but being conservative, our client was concerned about any possible negative reaction, so we took out a liability insurance policy for this event. The record company planned to pour honey all over Miss Wild Honey and blow feathers on her; then we would have the drawing to see which deejay would win and begin picking the feathers off (a silly concept, but newsworthy in the '50s). The Los Angeles area disc jockeys who participated were very popular and competitive at the time, including Peter Potter and Dick Haynes from KLAC, and Larry Finlay from KFWB, before it became an all-news station.

We hired very attractive, wholesome actress/models to appear as the various Miss Honeys. Miss Wild Honey was paid $50 and the other Honeys were paid $25 each (which was big bucks back then!). Miss Superior Honey, the daughter of a very well-known doctor, received an extra $25 because of what happened at our event.

The promoters had the winning deejay pour the honey over Miss Wild Honey (Marguerite Barbera). But he went against our wishes. Instead of pouring it on her shoulders and her bathing suit, as we had planned, the deejay poured the gooey substance over her head. Can you imagine the photo opportunity of that? We knew that honey is water soluble, so we weren't worried about any bad sticking affects. We just never dreamed they would pour the honey on her head! Fortunately, she was an actress and model looking for all the publicity she could get. When she was covered with honey—and the cameras were flashing lights all over the place —she instinctively jumped into the pool to get the sticky mess off her. She then ran into the hotel to take a shower and wash her hair. It caused quite a buzz, let me tell you. At least, everyone was having a good time and the deejays certainly were going to have plenty to talk about on their radio shows. It was fun up until what happened next.

While Miss Wild Honey was cleaning up, the then very important Associated Press cameraman showed up after the whole fracas was over and he was very upset that he had arrived too late. He asked us if we could re-enact everything for him! Here was a big, national publicity break for us. Since Miss Wild Honey was showering, I suggested we use Miss Superior Honey. We went over and asked her if she would do the whole routine for the Associated Press. To our relief she said "yes." We felt it wasn't fair for her to do it for free, so we asked our client if he would come up with an additional $25 for her extra work. The client agreed, because by now, he was really into the spirit of the event and his big buyers were happy that they

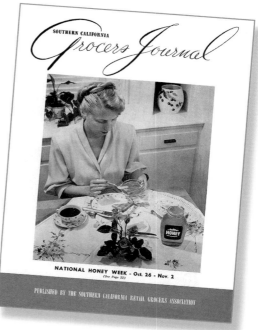

Grocers Journal cover featuring honey with the wife of the B-Z-B Honey Co. (see article on opposite page).

JOHN ARCESI lets go with the honey on model Eleanor Benvenesti. Disc jockeys Maurice Hart, Dick Haynes and Bill Leyden stand by for support. Stunt celebrated Arcesi's "Wild Honey" disc and National Honey Week. After she was honied, Miss Benvenesti was completely feathered.

were involved in this "Hollywood" activity. They did the whole bit over with Eleanor Benvenesti, Miss Superior Honey. Associated Press had its private media event and, as a result, national and international TV news shows picked up Miss Superior Honey instead of Miss Wild Honey in the photos and on television. What a break for her and what a break for us and our client!

A year later, we received a phone call from a friend who was watching the news on TV and said, "Did you know that Miss Wild Honey is suing everybody who was involved in the honey-and-feather party, for $70,000?" My jaw dropped. In her complaint, she said that "the duties for which she was hired consisted only of wearing a bathing suit and walking around the pool, and that nothing was said about honey being poured over her head." It was great publicity for her, because it appeared on every TV station and in all the newspapers. Many people were involved, including the deejays and Capitol Records' publicity department. Lee & Associates and I were not mentioned; however, she did include the Superior Honey Company. It was a good thing we had taken out that liability insurance policy! But, our insurance company and our client considered it a frivolous lawsuit. We learned that she just wanted the publicity. She was upset

Honey and feathers—a rare combination.

☆ ☆

that Eleanor had gotten all of the attention while she was showering. Capitol Records, being used to such things, was not concerned at all, and after various discussions with the lawyers, and after she got her publicity, they canceled the lawsuit and Capitol Records and the Superior Honey company each paid $70 apiece—incredible!

Like the proverbial "fly in the ointment," our wild honey caper had a few bugs in it. But all the extra publicity made everyone happy, and all was well in the worlds of honey, records and public relations.

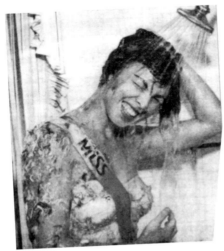

*The press photographers
even shot the cleanup.*

Model Seeks Damages for Honey and Feathers

First came the honey, then the feathers—Marguerite Barbera, 19, shuddered yesterday when she thought about it as she signed a $70,000 damage suit over her experience.

The complaint said that Miss Barbera, a tall and willowy model, was employed last Oct. 23 for a publicity stunt. She said she understood that her duties would consist only of donning a sketchy bathing suit and walking around the pool of a Hollywood hotel while a musical record of a crooner's voice was made.

Doused With Honey

But much to her chagrin and embarrassment, she said, suddenly a keg of honey was poured over her head and that was followed by a shower of feathers. She complained she was covered with the combination "from the crown of my head to the soles of my feet."

Her complaint, prepared by Atty. Bernard Lehrer, was directed against John Arcesi, the crooner; Pete Potter, disk jockey; Capitol Records, Inc; two press agents, Bud Freeman and Ed Scofield, and the Superior Honey Co. Miss Barbera sued through her mother, Mrs. Jeannette Barbera, 6028 Romain St.

At the time, Miss Barbera explained, she was playing the role of Miss Wild Honey and a recording of a song by the same name was in progress. The stunt was designed to publicize both the song and the product.

SUES — Miss Marguerite Barbera files honey and feather suit.

Times photo

*A year later and our
promotion was still in
the news.*

16

The Real Mrs. Cubbison

☆ ☆

"It's a match made in heaven." How often we hear that expression applied to relationships that are just the right "fit." They are rare, and therefore priceless, especially in business today. It is rarer still if such relationships endure for over a half-century. I was fortunate enough to have just such a business association with one of the finest people I've ever known, Mrs. Sophie Cubbison. For those of you who live in the western half of America, you would know her best as the creator of Mrs. Cubbison's Dressing Mix, which practically every family uses with their turkey at holiday time. Yes, Mrs. Cubbison was actually, quite a real person, who was a pioneer in establishing pre-packaged stuffing mixes as an alternative to home-prepared turkey dressing.

When I first branched out on my own in the public relations and advertising business, I was handling the California Turkey Advisory Board's publicity, and it was my task to "talk turkey" to the public. I

Mrs. Sophie Cubbison, a formidable person and businesswoman, taught America a better way to make stuffing in the early 1950s.

An early Mrs. Cubbison's ad (greatly enlarged).

was looking for ways to promote turkey as a meat that is excellent anytime, not just during the holiday season. While reading trade journals and newspapers, I kept noticing small—really small—two-inch ads that read "Turkey tastes great with Mrs. Cubbison's ready-to-use poultry dressing." It was almost like a very understated turn of the century (1900s, that is) advertisement, geared only to homemakers who were already familiar with the product, and had only to be reminded of it.

I saw the dressing mix prominently displayed in the markets at Thanksgiving time, and an idea struck me. I was trying to promote turkey as a year-round meat, so why not promote the dressing as a year-round item also? I contacted the company and learned that there really was a Mrs. Cubbison; she wasn't just an image. Not only did she exist, but she was fast becoming a household name, through the popularity of her products. The name on her products was real, not fictitious like "Betty Crocker." Over the years that I was privileged to know and work with her, I would come to admire Mrs. Sophie Cubbison for the American phenomenon and California pioneer that she was: a woman who starts a business in her kitchen and perseveres to become a leader of industry. She was an excellent cook and, as far as I know, she was one of the first top level women executives in the country.

Women of the 21st century may find

her story quite interesting, for Sophie Cubbison was a very modern young woman nearly 100 years ago. Born Sophie Huchting in San Marcos, California, in 1890, she was one of 10 children. Her father was of German descent and her mother was a native Californian of Mexican descent. In fact, her mother descended from the Ortega family, who were early California pioneers. Young Sophie became bent on a vocation at a very early age. As she once told me: "My career began on my father's ranch in San Diego County where I was born. At the age of 16, I started to cook for my father, brothers, and their lima-bean ranch laborers during the summer and early fall, so I could earn enough money to put myself through college." Sophie went on to earn a degree in home economics from California Polytechnic University in 1912, an era when most women never even pursued, or were permitted to pursue, higher education, much less acquire a degree.

But Sophie got quite an education on the ranch, as well. She was a wonderful example of someone who combines formal education with hands-on skill. "With one assistant, I cooked and baked for 40 men in two mobile kitchens," she once explained. "As the lima-bean harvest progressed through the day, the mobile kitchens were horse drawn, once or twice a day, to stay near the harvester. This was done for the convenience of the laborers at mealtimes; five times a day. Breakfast was served at 5 a.m., coffee break with a sweet snack at 9 a.m., dinner at 12 o'clock, coffee break and snack again at 4 p.m. and supper at 8:30 p.m." Sophie was there to prepare it all. Since the wholesale bakeries were not equipped to make country deliveries in those days, she baked all the necessary cakes, doughnuts, cookies and cupcakes. As Sophie so modestly put it, "I did not have mechanical kitchen equipment in those days; all the mixing was done manually." Here was a woman truly dedicated to her culinary art.

In 1913, Sophie began dating Harry Cubbison who was supporting his invalid father and mother. By this time, Sophie was supporting her mother, as her father had passed on. "Necessity became the mother of invention," Sophie told me. "Mr. Cubbison was a fine salesman and I was capable of baking. It was absolutely necessary for us to earn more money." After the couple married, Sophie became the Mrs. Cubbison whose products would one day embellish many a holiday dinner.

She and Harry went into debt to open a small bakery, and her entrepreneurial spirit rose to the occasion. A health enthusiast, she believed very strongly in whole wheat bread and Melba toast, especially. "To

☆ ☆

begin," Sophie recalled to me, "I would bake Cubbison's whole wheat bread three times a week, and on three other days I would go out and demonstrate the bread in stores and delicatessens. Mr. Cubbison did the soliciting and delivering."

Their venture met with success, and Sophie began to try her hand at baking Melba toast. In all of her "spare time" on the weekends, Sophie experimented in her kitchen with the wafer-thin bread that is slowly dried out in the oven. Like most culinary operations, the correct toasting of bread is something of a fine art. Good toast has been called "bread at its best." It is so popular in this country, in fact, that about one-third of our nation's bread is consumed in the form of toast. Thorough toasting of bread makes it easy to digest and brings about advantageous changes in its proteins.

History tells us that Melba toast is named after an opera diva named Nellie Melba who would order a "thin, dry toast" while staying in the Waldorf-Astoria in New York. She was ill, and the toast became part of her health regime because it aided digestion and was low in fat. One might say that, as a "toast" to Nellie, the wafers soon became known as Melba toast. By 1926, the Cubbison Melba Toast and Cracker Company was enjoying a modest success; but before long, a big break came their way.

While the nation was reeling from the 1929 stock market crash that would plunge America into the devastating economic depression of the 1930s—Sophie and Harry struck a bonanza. The famous "18-day reducing diet"—which included Melba toast—had been prescribed for actress Ethel Barrymore by the Mayo Brothers Clinic and was printed by most of the leading newspapers in the United States. Afterward, the demand for Melba toast became so great, the Cubbisons were forced to operate three plants for the next 18 months to meet the popular demand. This is an example of how powerful even unplanned publicity can be.

Soon, Sophie was using Melba toast as a substitute in recipes that called for bread crumbs. She also began using it for stuffing turkeys and other fowl. "Friends and relatives dining with us from time-to-time would rave about my dressing and ask for my recipe." A bell began to ring—Mrs. Cubbison's Poultry Dressing and Corn Bread Stuffin' mixes were potential products for the food markets! That's how Mrs. Cubbison's most famous products were introduced. Over the next several decades, they have had outstanding success, and continue to be even more popular in this new century.

☆ ☆

I came into the picture about 1950 when I followed up on one of her small ads that I kept seeing in newspapers. I suggested that, since she was promoting dressing and I was promoting turkeys, we should work together. Little did I realize this was the beginning of a great, very long relationship. Mrs. Cubbison had a small Melba toast bread factory in downtown Los Angeles, at that time. She had two brothers working for her in the sales department, and was running the business with 14 driver/salesmen delivering Melba toast and stuffing mix to the markets.

She soon hired my agency and I began doing advertising and public relations for her company. We energetically sought plausible ways to combine stuffing and turkey, especially for all the holidays. The first year, we created special events featuring cooking demonstrations. We placed Sophie on every possible radio and television show, and we arranged for her to visit with newspaper and magazine food editors. They used Sophie's recipes and food photos, and gradually she became well known in the media. Showing her strong pioneer spirit, she proved to be a very adamant, talented hard-worker. As a client, she was very savvy because she knew, even then, that you can't sell dressing by itself. You have to sell the whole meal. She was very gracious about telling people all the things that could be done with dressing, as well as conveying other tips to enhance holiday meals. That's how Mrs. Cubbison's became the traditional Thanksgiving turkey dressing mix.

Together, Sophie and I, and my then-small staff, were promoting

Mrs. Cubbison's small fleet of trucks in the late 1930s—
Leo would later promote her fine products for the next 50 plus years.

*Melba toast was a
hot product in the 1920s.*

*Sophie was interested in
healthy foods even before
this 1920s photo.*

turkeys and dressing, day-in and day-out. I coined the phrase: "Anytime is turkey time." Sophie came up with the term: "planned-overs," instead of "leftovers." We came up with several slogans which are still being used today: "It wouldn't be a holiday without Mrs. Cubbison's." "It's Melba toasted." "It's seasoned just right." "Mrs. Cubbison's makes the best turkey taste even better!"

We created recipe leaflets featuring not only turkeys and dressing, but also many ideas for the entire meal. We wanted to give the homemaker inventive choices, and encourage their own creativity in planning meals or parties. Sophie's winning philosophy was that, when you make a food product, you have to think of the mass public. She used basic spices to enhance the taste of her dressing mix. Then she and I made suggestions to homemakers on how to glamorize the dressing by adding their own favorite ingredients, such as raisins, chopped carrots, celery, onion, nuts, chopped prunes, or whatever. Our recipes encouraged food artistry among homemakers.

During the 1950s, when television was still quite a new invention, practically every television station had a food show. Sophie became a regular on these cooking shows that, as we see on cable television today, had many likable, "homey" kitchen personalities. Here, in Southern California, we had Chef Milani, Mama Weiss, Mercedes Gaffney, Freida Nelson,

☆ ☆ ☆ ☆ ☆ ☆ ☆ ☆ ☆ ☆ ☆ ☆ ☆ ☆ ☆ ☆ ☆ ☆ ☆ ☆

and Mercedes Bates, who later became General Mills' Betty Crocker. In addition, there were many women's interest shows and farm shows on radio.

Who doesn't know of Bob Barker, host of the longest running TV game show, "The Price is Right," for over 28 years? Mrs. Cubbison's products, to a small degree, figured into Bob's fantastic career as an enduring and endearing game show host. In 1951, Bob and his wife, Dorothy Jo, had a local radio program sponsored by the Southern California Edison Company. Edison, a local utility company, sponsored "Electric Living Centers" in cities around the Los Angeles area. The Edison offices had auditoriums in which the centers were set up, and programs were held to entice women to attend cooking classes and demonstrations of electric appliances, such as freezers. Bob and Dorothy Jo would show the appliances and then do the radio program afterward, there in one of the Edison auditoriums. Lee & Associates supplied gift packs of our clients' products for Bob and his wife to use as prizes and as part of their presentation. I remember the two of them driving up to our office in their Studebaker, to pick up the packages. I helped load the car with Mrs. Cubbison's Dressing Mix and other products, and gave them plenty of recipes and serving suggestions. I don't know how it all fit in the car with them; they were both very tall people! Somehow they made it back to the Edison auditoriums and their audiences, which averaged between 75-100 attendees. Soon, homemak-

Bob Barker during his early years—and still going strong.

An early 1950s Edison Auditorium show promoting home use of electricity.

ers throughout Los Angeles County were learning all about Mrs. Cubbison's products on Bob and Dorothy's radio show. Bob recently reminisced to me about those years. "You know, we gave away so many Mrs. Cubbison's products on that show, I'm surprised anyone was left to buy them," he chuckled.

As a result of those delightful and informative radio programs, Bob's career took off in 1957. Noted television game show producer Ralph Edwards had created a new program called "Truth or Consequences." Game shows were becoming very hot in the late 1950s. Edwards sold the program to NBC as a daytime show, but he hadn't found the master of ceremonies that he wanted. One day while driving, he turned on KNX radio in Los Angeles and happened to hear one of the Edison programs that Bob and Dorothy Jo hosted. "Fortunately for me," Bob recalled, "I was called in for an audition; then everything changed." Bob won national fame as the popular host on the "Truth or Consequences" game show, which aired for the next 18 years. Bob didn't stop there. He went on to host "The Price Is Right," the longest running game show in television history. "Dorothy always said I was nothing, if not tenacious," Bob recently quipped.

Bob's beloved Dorothy Jo died in 1981,

☆ ☆

but her memory lives on in the "DJ and T Foundation" started by Bob. Named in honor of Dorothy Jo and Bob's mother Tillie, the foundation funds grants for low-cost or free spaying and neutering for animal clinics all over the nation. Bob was featured on the Arts & Entertainment TV network's popular "Biography" series. We all know Bob as the host who popularized the phrase, "Come on down!" But I will always have special memories of him as that young man in his Studebaker loaded up with Mrs. Cubbison's gift packs.

As television was gaining in popularity in the 1950s, we found other opportunities to promote Mrs. Cubbison's products. We even decided to have Sophie appear on children's shows. This was a first. But Sophie was the grandmother type, so that made her a natural with kids. More often than not, children will listen to their grandparents more than their parents. We came up with ideas for her to go on the children's shows and tell stories about food—mostly turkeys—especially during holiday times. Many of you may recall, children's programming in the 1950s was hosted by a variety of appealing personalities. I developed lasting friendships with such kiddie notables as Sheriff John, Tom Hatten, Engineer Bill, Skipper Frank, Billy Barty, Miss Frances of "The Romper Room," Captain Jet and Bozo the Clown. These kid-show hosts would stir up a little excitement by saying something like, "Hey kids! Get mom in to watch Sophie Cubbison! She's got lots of good things to tell us about how to cook!" With any luck, grandma would be watching, too! On occasion, we would even arrange for the TV production crew to visit a turkey ranch, so that Sophie could talk about the Pilgrims and our Thanksgiving Day tradition. Of course, she would talk about the dressing.

We didn't just get her good exposure in the media. Our promotion took us in every conceivable direction. We covered many other bases. In those days, many cooking schools were sponsored by the Southern California Gas Company, the Los Angeles Department of Water and Power, and Southern California Edison. So we made arrangements to have Sophie appear as a celebrity guest demonstrator. Then, we would distribute recipes and write publicity stories about the events to send out to the local media. Sophie would also go with us to the state and county fairs where she would spend several days judging contests and putting on cooking demonstrations. You know, audiences would keep asking us about the difference between dressing and stuffing. Actually, they are one and the same, but historically, it is referred to as "stuffing" on the East coast and "dressing" on the west coast.

☆ ☆

I think we must have taught the whole world how to prepare and stuff turkeys, and make dressing as a side dish. We believed in the tradition of public relations, that, with this type of product, the "third person" word-of-mouth endorsement would do more for us than anything else. That's what motivated us. We dealt with home economists, providing them with literature, samples, recipes, and serving suggestions. We prepared lesson plans and academic information for cooking schools, not just for turkeys, but for all types of main entrées, with which dressing could be used. We even arranged for the U.S. Army to have our home economist go to Fort Ord to teach their cooks how to prepare turkey, to make it taste as close to "homemade" as possible, so soldiers could feel as if they were getting a home-cooked meal.

Sophie's husband Harry died in 1953. Not long afterward, Sophie sold her bakery in 1955 to the American Cone and Pretzel Company, which later became Rold Gold Pretzels. She was beginning to have health problems, and running a business without Harry was quite a strain, but she did agree to stay on with the company as a consultant. However, she insisted that the buyer retain Lee & Associates as its advertising and public relations agency, or she would not complete the sale, telling the buyer that we had helped her increase her business to the point where it was profitable to sell. Naturally, the buyer honored her wishes, even though they could have eventually let us go. We've now been promoting Mrs. Cubbison's products for over 50 years. I rarely see this kind of loyalty in business today. I think that's a shame, in many ways. Over the years, five mergers have occurred since Mrs. Cubbison originally sold her company, and we have remained the public relations and advertising agency for Mrs. Cubbison's products each time. We do not know of more than one or two other agencies in the country that have had an account for that long. The Foote, Cone and Belding advertising agency has had the Sunkist account since 1907, which I believe is the oldest agency relationship, spanning nearly a century.

Sophie remained an active consultant to the company to make sure her namesake continued to represent a high quality product. When not traveling around the world, she would visit the markets to observe how her products were placed, and she would even call us with recipes she had discovered during her travels. Sophie maintained her friendship with us and the buyer of the company. She kept in touch for many years, giving advice, adding new recipes, and keeping us informed about markets she visited during her travels and whether they carried her products. Mrs. Cubbison remained an active consultant through the 1960s and early 1970s, until her declining health caused her to become less active.

Interstate Bakeries Corporation (which owns several different brands of bread and cake products such as Wonder Bread and Hostess) bought the business, which is now known as Mrs. Cubbison's Foods, Inc. Interstate Bakeries is now the largest independent bakery company in the United States.

Ron Parque (l.), president of Mrs. Cubbison's Foods, briefing actor Dennis Weaver on the nuances of dressing mix, before an early 1980s radio commercial recording session.

Mrs. Cubbison's Foods has adhered to the age-old adage, "If it ain't broke, don't fix it," and therefore continues to be successful by using Sophie's basic formula. Mrs. Cubbison's Foods President, Ron Parque, carries on Sophie's legacy, and has this to say about the firm's continued growth: "For many months prior to the holiday season, we bake over 65,000 loaves of fresh, specially-formulated bread daily, to be transformed into the millions of boxes of Mrs. Cubbison's turkey dressing products, primarily sold in the western United States, and throughout the country. We stick to Sophie's basic, original recipe, which has proven to be the real success behind her popular products."

Sophie Cubbison passed away in 1982 at the age of 92, ironically, just after the Thanksgiving holiday when her dressing and stuffing mixes dominate the grocery shelves.

☆ ☆

As you will read in the following chapter, we occasionally send our clients' products to the prop departments at movie and TV studios, to hopefully appear in a scene or two. We had a tremendously good break when one of our propman friends said he had a movie coming up that had to do with a supermarket scene. He said he couldn't guarantee anything, but he needed lots of food products to display on the movie set's grocery shelves. We delivered many products to the movie studio, especially Mrs. Cubbison's, which were the bulkiest packages, yet the easiest to handle because of their light weight. National brands also have a better chance for long, up-front exposure.

The movie turned out to be none other than Warner Brothers' phenomenally successful "Oh God!" starring George Burns and John Denver. We found out later that the supermarket scene, with which we had helped the prop department by supplying all those groceries, was a very important part of the story. When John Denver, who played a supermarket checker, was loading groceries at the check stand in the movie's opening scene, picked up the Mrs. Cubbison's Stuffin' box—there it was, bigger than life on the screen. Of course, it became a complete billboard for us. It is the type of thing we in the public relations business dream about. Naturally, we contacted our client, the food brokers and salespeo-

John Denver was their star and Mrs. Cubbison's Stuffin' Mix (on counter) was our star, in the hit movie "Oh, God."

☆ ☆

ple who worked for us, and told them to go see "Oh God!" and look for the Mrs. Cubbison's package so prominently displayed. If advertising is "paying," and public relations is "praying," then somebody upstairs had certainly been listening to us!

The amazing thing was that, when the movie came out, we received dozens of phone calls from friends who knew that we handled the Mrs. Cubbison's food account. They said to us, "Did you know that Mrs. Cubbison's is in 'Oh God!?'" Talk about great publicity!

We used the photograph from that movie scene for years to impress the sales force and the retailers when we talked about the exposure we obtained for Mrs. Cubbison's. We stressed to them the importance of product placements in movies, which in this case became an invaluable tool. It was wonderful. "Oh God!" netted $30 million in 1977, a huge amount of money, back then, and became so popular, it spawned two sequels, not to mention the video sales and rentals that will be with us forever. Also, it has been on TV many times, seen by many millions of potential purchasers of Mrs. Cubbison's products.

I thank heaven for this "match made in heaven," my long-time association with the creative and dedicated Mrs. Cubbison, and the company so devoted to preserving her successful formula. I started out with Sophie Cubbison when her advertising consisted of two-inch newspaper and magazine ads, and I helped boost her company all the way to where it became the most popular holiday dressing in the country. I watched her company grow and develop over the years, and now Mrs. Cubbison Foods, Inc. has their own website at www.mrscubbisons.com, with lots of turkey and dressing recipes and handy cooking hints. Although Mrs. Cubbison's was originally distributed in the Western United States, now the company has expanded eastward and added a complete line of croutons that rank as number one in sales across the nation.

The recipes that she developed, and her concept of cooking, are still being used today. The products continue to maintain the tradition and high standards that Sophie Cubbison developed all those years ago. I sincerely wish everyone's business associations could be as rewarding and enduring as mine has been with Mrs. Cubbison.

17

Movie & TV Tie-Ins — From "Rocky" to "Friends"

☆ ☆

While most public relations professionals enter the field through their writing ability, usually with a journalism background, I entered the business because of my education in marketing and my background in television. Today, students are receiving degrees in public relations from many top universities and colleges throughout the country.

About 1950, while working with Eddie Bracken at Bracken Television Productions, I become acquainted with the producers, directors and other personnel involved in television, movies and radio. I found if I could provide props or product information useful to the television and film industry—or if I could entertain, inform or cause some excitement through my clients' products—a way then existed for all of us to work together. One rule that I established is that I wanted to create long-term relationships. Anything Lee & Associates provided or created had to be as good for the movie and television people as it was for us, because we would be coming back again and again to the studios with another client's product or another project to promote, and we would never abuse the privilege. In those days, and from then on, it was important for us to build a relationship and show reliability and stability. It is a wonderful feeling. We developed many contacts and fine friends that have lasted for years, and we have accomplished a great deal. These movie and television promotional "tie-ins" led us on many adventures, as I will recount in this chapter.

A "Rocky" Opportunity

One of my more memorable experiences is what I call "The Rocky Episode." It was unbelievable. One day in the mid-1970s, I got a phone call from a promoter who was hired by a movie producer to raise as much money as possible to help with a particular film's production costs. The promoter had heard that we were handling publicity for Suntory Whiskey, and he suggested that we had an opportunity to get good exposure for Suntory in this new movie about an unknown boxer. This film turned out to be the blockbuster that put a little-known actor named Sylvester Stallone on the movie star map. It was called "Rocky," and at the

☆ ☆

time, the proposed film was something of a "rocky" venture.

First off, I asked to see the script. He showed me a scene, set in Philadelphia, when the boxer would be wearing a robe. He made me an offer; "I would essentially like to have Suntory Whiskey 'buy the space' and have its name printed on the back of the robe, for $50,000."

I choked back a gasp, then I said to him: "That's more money than we have ever had for our entire Suntory budget, plus it seems totally incongruous to me that a boxer in Philadelphia would have Japanese whiskey as a sponsor on the back of his robe." But all was not lost, so I continued on with the promoter. "However, we sure would like to work with you; let's see what we can do."

I knew that he was desperate to keep the film's production costs down. The scene was coming up within a week, and he was calling everyone in town who was looking for exposure for their clients' products. Every day he called, he dropped his price. In a few days, he was finally down to $5,000 for the back-of-the-robe advertisement.

At that time, we were also handling the Binaca breath-refresher spray. I thought "Rocky' would be much better exposure for Binaca. What I envisioned fit in more with the movie's theme: I could just see the company's slogan emblazoned on the back of Stallone's robe, "The Binaca Blast." Incidentally, Sylvester Stallone was then an unknown factor, but I got excited when I read the script because I thought it was a great movie! Little did I realize how big Stallone would become after this movie's release. So, I called the president of Binaca and said I thought this would be a great deal. He told me that his budget was already stretched for the year and just couldn't handle it; he would have to pass it up. I was devastated. I even suggested that we cancel several of our TV game show plugs and use that money, because I felt this movie had a big future; and he still said "no." Undeterred, I then suggested that we would just take the money out of the regular funds we had available for future game show promotions. The only response I got from him was "No, no, no."

I offered the opportunity to another client. I called the vice president of public relations at Frito-Lay, a good friend of mine. I was so excited about the "Rocky" opportunity, I even called him at home, telling him this would be a fantastic placement for Fritos corn chips. The Fritos public relations department was completely out of money for the year, so we had to go to their marketing department. I called and pleaded and begged them to do it, and they said, "no dice."

☆ ☆

Here we had this terrific opportunity that everyone was passing up. Our two clients who could most benefit from it had said "no." My professional pride was hurt, but you don't go telling your clients that they are wrong—even if you would like to. So, I went back to the "Rocky" promoter and told him we couldn't come up with the money.

The promoter wound up putting Rocky's brother-in-law's meat-packing company name on the back of the robe. In other words, nobody bought this valuable space. What an unbelievable opportunity wasted! Every time I see a rerun of the movie on TV, and the scene comes on in which Rocky enters the boxing ring with his robe on, I keep thinking how I could have had a client's product name on it for only $5,000. Today, they would probably pay over $100,000 for that kind of exposure.

Another opportunity sprang up in the film. The big fight scene was going to take place in a sports arena, and the film company would have hundreds of extras in the seats. The film's promoter, who had previous experience with rock concerts, made a deal with local Los Angeles radio station KHJ. He asked the station to announce to the public that, anyone who wanted to see a free boxing match and be in a movie scene should come to the Los Angeles Sports Arena on the designated day. They would also be given some snacks to eat, since they would be there the better part of a day. So, the promoter was getting film extras for free, and he would now need food to feed them.

That's when a couple of ideas occurred to me. A scene in the script called for Rocky to gulp down raw eggs, for added strength. So I told the promoter: "I also represent the egg industry. I can get you 1,000 hard-cooked eggs for your extras, if you let my staff take publicity pictures and get some exposure on KHJ radio." I envisioned 1,000 film extras eating hard-cooked eggs while watching this boxing match. I'm sure everyone recalls that memorable scene when Rocky gulps down the raw eggs.

I negotiated to give the promoter 1,000 packages of Fritos if he would allow us to take publicity photographs and also get us favorable exposure on radio. I also asked that a Fritos sign be placed somewhere in the sports arena during filming. After all, when you have a boxing match, you have to have signs posted to make it look realistic. They put a little sign reading "Fritos" above one of the doors in the scene, so that it would be picked up by the camera. By the way, all of this took place on very short notice. With my sons Howard and Frank, I loaded up our station wagon and another car with the hard-cooked eggs and we had the Fritos delivered. We drove down to the arena and got involved with the many hundreds of movie extras. Several coordinators with bullhorns shouted out to one section of the audience at a time to come over and get the free snacks and sodas which were being handed out. Actually, it was done quite orderly, considering how many people there were to serve.

It was curious to watch a film being made with extras. Periodically, they were moved from one section of the sports arena to another, to make it appear on film as if there were thousands of people in the audience. It is one more optical illusion in the film industry's bag of tricks (today, it's all done with computer animation). The venture was exciting for us and, as you know, "Rocky" really took off! It was so successful, it spawned three more sequels and Sylvester Stallone certainly became a mega-superstar. I really acquired a great deal of respect for the "Rocky" production team. They were smart people. They started on a shoestring budget and managed to complete their project successfully.

Human nature, being what it is, I was tempted to say, "I told you so" to my clients who "passed" on the incredible opportunity I offered them. But I never said a word, and called it a day. I'm sure they have seen the movie several times, by now.

"Dressed to the Nines" in Aluminum Foil

We all know how creative one can get with aluminum foil. We use it for just about everything outside its intended use as a wrap to keep food fresh. We cover soda cans with it when we put them back in the refrigerator, we use it to wrap half-eaten sandwiches, and we even make origami shapes out of it. Why, some people even use it as a substitute for window shades! As far as I know, the aluminum foil fashion show with which I got involved was a first. In the early 1950s, Lee & Associates was chosen to create publicity in California for Alcoa, the famous makers of aluminum foil. Alcoa had a complete staff of public relations representatives, and two very large advertising agencies, but they were still unable to make a dent in the California market with their aluminum foil. Kaiser and Reynolds aluminum products dominated the market at that time. When Alcoa hired us to do regional public relations, we used all the usual publicity techniques we could think up. Many of them worked, such as encouraging the public to use Alcoa aluminum foil during summer barbecuing activities (Californians love barbecues), to wrap school lunch sandwiches, and so on.

We were looking for other attention-getting devices to attract the media, when I discovered that Alcoa had at one time created a fashion

☆ ☆

show in tandem with another event. It had featured women's dresses and bathing suits made out of aluminum thread. You can imagine that these designs were pretty glitzy. They were high-fashion creations that had a very special glow all their own. The company had not done much about promoting the glittering clothing, so I obtained the dresses and bathing suits and began developing my own ideas about a fashion show.

We decided to create a fashion extravaganza that would really catch the media's attention. There's certainly no question it would dazzle everyone's eyes. I went over to local Los Angeles independent television station, KTTV, and asked if we could stage the show on one of their programs. The first show in the morning aired at 8 a.m., this being long before the days of 24-hour programing. (In the early days of television, stations usually signed off the air right after midnight and did not come back on until early in the morning.) We offered to pay a very modest charge—I don't think it was more than $200—to have them put on the show with Bill Welch and Norma Gilchrist, who were much like our morning talk show hosts today. I agreed to communicate with all the local grocers and have them watch the show. This would give KTTV very good exposure to the grocery industry, with whom they were always anxious to work.

The promotional gimmick we created had never been done before.

An attractive model dramatizing the strength of heavy-duty Alcoa Aluminum Wrap.

☆ ☆

We didn't know how it would all turn out. Nevertheless, we went ahead and put the fashion show together and included a contest for the grocers to enter. Therefore, the show was targeting the grocers, not the consumers. We sent out direct-mail advertisements, bulletins, and post cards, advising the grocers that we had a special program coming up on KTTV just for them. One of the grocers could also win a trip to Hawaii. It was a gimmick. We had no idea how many people would watch. We called around to the grocers, and they told us the whole thing was so crazy that they thought it was actually a good idea.

Bill Welch and Norma Gilchrist were both popular daytime TV personalities, so we anticipated a good-sized audience would tune in that normally would not be watching at that time. We hired the most beautiful models we could find to wear the sparkling fashions, which really were sensational. We had the participating grocers send in cards if they were going to watch. We would have a drawing during the show, and if the winner was watching, he or she would get the prize. It was very exciting and we certainly got our message across about aluminum foil. I wonder how many dressmakers in the viewing audience began ordering aluminum thread? Plus, I think because of our contest, KTTV got the idea to air food-related programs at earlier hours. The advertising manager of Shopping Bag Market (which merged later with Vons), Shep Aparicio, won the trip to Hawaii. He was quite flabbergasted, as it was an unexpected surprise for him. The reaction from many of the grocers was

Los Angeles TV station, KTTV, became a focal point for local grocers, to introduce them to Alcoa's product with an "aluminum fashion show," in the early 1950's.

great. The ones who were not able to watch our special TV show heard about it from the ones who did. This helped get a good deal of attention for Alcoa aluminum foil with the grocers and many consumers.

Jerry Lewis Team Goes "Nutty" for Peanuts

One of our biggest successes was one where we made no money, but did make some good friends. Building up business relationships is vital. The bottom line is not always about instant cash and a "hard sell." In the early 1960s, the publicist at Paramount Studios heard that we had supplied pretzels for a movie called "It's a Mad, Mad, Mad, Mad World." The studio's publicity department called to ask if we also had peanuts, because they were making a movie with Jerry Lewis called the "The Nutty Professor," which subsequently became quite a hit with audiences. So popular, in fact, that talented comedian/actor Eddie Murphy starred in two "Nutty Professor" films nearly forty years later. The Jerry Lewis production team was very promotion-minded and always receptive to any legitimate means of getting additional publicity for his films.

Steve Shagan, who was in charge of publicity at Paramount (he later became a leading film producer and successful author), was open to our suggestions. I brought him together with Roy Fishman, who was public relations director for Standard Brands, which marketed popular Planter's Peanuts. I did a favor for two people, with the result that we worked out a method of exposure that was beneficial to both the studio and the peanut marketer. Standard Brands put a promotion on their peanut bags, millions of bags, drawing attention to the movie, "The Nutty Professor." Planter's Peanuts were visibly seen displayed in this successful film. We were able to have the popular costumed character, "Mr. Peanut," appear at several very big movie premieres, getting us lots of exposure for Planter's Peanuts. No money was exchanged, we made two companies very happy, we made new friends and, subsequently, both Paramount Studios and Standard Brands were quite favorable to our future promotional tie-ins.

Rolling in the (Tortilla) Chips

Building on success, I used the example of what we accomplished with Planter's when I contacted a publicist at each of the major studios. I told them to call me when they were looking for additional media exposure, because I could get them Frito-Lay tortilla chips and other products to use in films. In return, I could promote their movies if I got the proper placement of my clients' products within their films. This led me on many film adventures over the years, but certain ones stand out.

☆ ☆ ☆ ☆ ☆ ☆ ☆ ☆ ☆ ☆ ☆ ☆ ☆ ☆ ☆ ☆ ☆ ☆ ☆ ☆

In 1979, Warner Brothers made a sci-fi movie about Jack The Ripper called "Time After Time," which brought the villain into the twentieth century via a time machine. The producers decided to show several things in the modern world that had not yet been invented in Jack's day (the 1800s). A scene included an airplane that was skywriting an advertisement and they needed a message for the skywriter to etch across the sky. We suggested that we would help promote the movie through all of our contacts, if they would use a Frito-Lay product name . We went back and forth in negotiations, finally ending up with the airplane spelling out "Doritos," one of the Frito-Lay brands of tortilla chips. The movie wasn't exactly "Gone With The Wind," but it was a great visual plug.

The First Health Foods Bar on a Movie Set

We were lucky in many of our dealings with the studios, because we represented healthy food products. In fact, one year it really paid off for us. An opportunity occurred that gave us a whole new outlet for informing the public about nutritional products, and it came about quite by accident. One day in 1967, I called Inge Jaklin, one of the models we often hired to promote our products, but she was unavailable for the assignment. She had a part in a new James Bond-type of spy movie being filmed at 20th Century Fox. So, I called Eve Bruce, another actress/model, but she, too, was unavailable, as she had a part in the same movie! They say the third time is the charm, but I struck out again when I called the third model on my list. She was unavailable because she was also working in the film. If I didn't know better, I would have

"In Like Flint" sports Hollywood's first on-set healthy juice bar.

suspected a conspiracy! Did everybody in Hollywood have a part in this new movie?

I got curious and asked about the film. I learned the new movie, "In Like Flint," starring James Coburn, was about a society of Amazon-type women, who were using a health resort as a front for their real mission; they were plotting to conquer the world. The movie was a sequel to the popular "Our Man Flint" spoof of the early "secret agent" movies.

James Coburn inspecting the California Prune Board's Award of Distinction to 20th Century Fox Studios, for allowing us to place the Health Bar on the set.

A great idea occurred to me—connect my clients' products with this movie's health-oriented theme. We had clients in the food industry with generic products. For example, boysenberries, honey, turkey, prunes and various dairy items, like certified raw milk. I contacted the publicity department at 20th Century Fox. I suggested that I could get a lot of publicity for them if, instead of the usual coffee-and-doughnuts bar that is on the movie set for the actors and crew, we establish a health-foods bar. Their publicists could write about the fact that 20th Century Fox movie employees, especially the attractive female stars, were having their morning break eating healthy foods. It worked. We received not only national, but also international coverage, especially in the fan magazines and movie columns, where that kind of movie publicity is very powerful. It was especially pleasing to have the opportunity to inform the whole world about good nutrition.

Celebrities Make Glamorous Cooks

One tie-in that I created, relating to film celebrities, involved "The TV-Movie News." This was a free publication, put out nationally by TV Fanfare Publications. It was published for about 10 years. Designed much like a larger, more slender version of "TV Guide," it was a weekly, listing the schedules of movies that were airing on television. The publication was delivered to 10,000 supermarkets throughout the country, with a circulation of five million copies. Each participating market had its own name and address printed on it, with other local merchants near the market subsidizing the publication. To relate it to the supermarkets, the editors needed recipes with different ingredients. We used the exposure for our various clients and celebrities. We agreed to supply the publication with recipes, while they supplied the photos of current celebrities, to add some glamour. This was favor payback time—we could now pay back celebrities who had helped us previously in various activities or by posing for food publicity photos. This supermarket TV magazine was excellent exposure for the celebrities, some of them up and coming, who later became bigger stars. They certainly enjoyed it. This is a fine example of how everyone benefited— the markets, the celebrities and our food industry clientele. My second book, "Recipes of the Stars" highlights many of these recipes (a few can be found here

Actress Francine York could make any dish look and taste glamorous.

in Chapter 22). The celebrity recipe book includes recipes from such favorite stars as Edward Asner, Burt Reynolds, Tony Randall, Howard Duff, Francine York, Lorne Greene, Irene Ryan, Jack La Lanne, Sid Caesar, Barbara Bain, Dinah Shore, Chelsea Brown, Richard Long, Juliet Mills, Fred MacMurray, Peter Graves, Henry Mancini, Wayne Newton, Diahann Carroll and many more.

More Media Outlets for Good Eating

The California Dairy Council had a successful campaign for "public service announcements," —short radio and TV messages that are available free to non-profit organizations. I created a public service radio concept for the Dairy Council; I offered to provide celebrities the opportunity to record public service announcements talking about good nutrition, which at that time included the "basic four food groups." We contacted many of the top talent agents to give them the opportunity of our fringe benefits of radio exposure. We worked directly with the public service directors on radio stations and made short news items, usually recorded at the studio where the celebrity was working. The celebrities were very gracious and a pleasure to work with. Their publicity agents were pleased with the added mass exposure for their clients and their latest movie, while we were getting exposure for our client's products. To name a few, we worked with such stars as Don Knotts, Jim Nabors, Phyllis

Don Knotts starred in the movie, "How to Frame a Figg"—a natural tie-in we couldn't resist—with our California Fig Advisory Board client.

☆ ☆ ☆ ☆ ☆ ☆ ☆ ☆ ☆ ☆ ☆ ☆ ☆ ☆ ☆ ☆ ☆ ☆ ☆ ☆

Diller, Sammy Davis, Jr., Bob Newhart, The Supremes, Jack Carter, Tom Jones and Don Adams.

Bill Cosby, in particular, was very nice. We worked with him on the Dairy Board and nutrition tie-in. We later found out he loves turkey. One Thanksgiving holiday, he helped us out a great deal. We decided to send out a Thanksgiving news release and accompanying photo featuring turkey, stuffing and prunes, and Bill agreed to pose with the products. We didn't mention any brand name in the story. We were happy just to get the media to write about the recipe. We kept the assignment strictly generic.

Bill Cosby poses with turkey, stuffing and prunes.

We sent the release and photo to our usual media outlets, though this time, because of the television connection with his popular "I Spy" series, we also sent it to NBC's media contacts. The results were terrific. We received many thousands of requests for Bill Cosby's turkey stuffing recipe (see chapter 22). NBC was also pleased with the exra exposure the "I Spy" series received in the food pages of many newspapers.

"Barnaby Jones," the popular detective series that starred legendary performer Buddy Ebsen, was a hot program in the early 1970s, and we supplied props for their many kitchen scenes. The "Barnaby Jones" refrigerators always had prune juice, prunes, Superior honey and even turkeys. In the background you would find Mrs. Cubbison's Dressing Mix and many more of our clients' products, such as Danish cheese, Armanino chives and even

Airwick air-freshener was set on top of the refrigerator.

In any business, it is very important to keep your contacts, through relationships that you build up over the years. We, in particular, developed those crucial relationships in various departments at the major TV and movie studios. My son, Howard, had a contact who was a high-ranking executive with Warner Brothers Television. A couple of months before the Thanksgiving holiday in 1995, Howard sent this executive a couple of cases of Mrs. Cubbison's product, reminding her that situation comedy scriptwriters were probably ready to start writing their holiday shows. Howard asked her to think about including scenes using dressing and turkey, giving him an opportunity to have a plug for Mrs. Cubbison's. She made no promises to Howard, but said that she would try to place the dressing boxes in the background on some of the shows that were taped at Warner Brothers studio.

We kept Barnaby Jones' fridge well-stocked with appropriate products, such as prune juice.

Sure enough, just before Thanksgiving, Howard happened to be watching the popular TV show "Friends," that at the time had the second largest viewing audience on television, with over 40 million viewers, just behind the "ER" series. Most of the "Friends" episodes centered around the characters in an apartment that had an open pantry of products on display. There, on the bottom shelf, was a box of Mrs.

Cubbison's Dressing Mix. The box remained on the program for a few weeks in a row. Boxes of the dressing appeared on a few other shows, as well. "Friends" is still very popular and has an even larger audience through reruns.

Howard would also communicate with the TV production and prop departments at many of the top shows and offer to help them create a Thanksgiving turkey scene. Prop personnel would call up a couple of weeks before Thanksgiving and say they were taping a Thanksgiving segment and had their own turkey, but they needed other items in the background, like our dressing mix. The box of dressing would end up as an integral part of the scene when the characters of the shows would be in the kitchen, with stories centered around cooking a turkey. Some of the popular shows on which we placed our Mrs. Cubbison's boxes have included "3rd Rock from the Sun," with John Lithgow, and "Suddenly Susan," starring Brooke Shields, "Felicity," starring Keri Russell, "Veronica's Closet," starring Kirstie Alley, and "Buffy the Vampire Slayer," which stars Sarah Michelle Geller. I guess even vampire slayers like to prepare a Thanksgiving meal and sink their teeth into turkey and dressing once in a while.

When one has been around Hollywood for as long as I have, it is interesting to note how interrelated the TV shows become, in terms of exchanging props. Our clients' products show up from time to time on some TV shows of which we are not even aware, because the prop person from one particular TV series may also be the same prop person for another series. We have viewed our clients' products transported from one TV family to another! At least we know our favorite TV families are eating wholesomely.

We worked with the prop personnel and the set decorators who had a problem when it came to filling up entire grocery stores or kitchen scenes. We developed a rapport with them, so they would call upon us as a source. Although we represented several food accounts, we could not fill up a whole grocery store, so we offered to help the prop department find all the products. We would call up our friends and colleagues in the food industry and ask them to supply items in their product line. Once in a while, one of our colleagues would also get a good break by having a close-up of their product with the show's star standing right beside it during a scene.

To help defray rising production costs, some of the producers eventually began asking for money for such product placements in movies and on television. It became a regular business with some contacts. Since it took between six and nine months, or even longer, to make a movie, the company that provided the product would never know if it was going to appear in the movie as agreed upon. Through a very complicated contract formula, if the product was not visible for more than a few seconds or not seriously recognizable, we would not pay. We didn't like to be asked to pay for a placement. We didn't encourage it with our clients and didn't seek to participate in that type of product promotion. Later on, as TV and movie audiences grew, product placement became BIG business, beginning in the 1980s. As I said, since we were not selling this type of service and were working with our own clients and friends, we were more anxious to develop long-term, friendly relationships with producers, set decorators, and prop departments to garner good exposure for our clients' products.

Several product placement companies popped up, doing nothing but reading hundreds of TV and movie scripts, while looking for every possible place in the story to plug a product. If a scene called for a character to get into a car, someone from each of these companies would call the appropriate car manufacturers. They had to decide if the character should drive an expensive sports car, a luxury sedan, a family van, or

In the 1975 movie, "The Sunshine Boys," Walter Mathau
is possibly wondering where the product tie-ins are—Can you find them?

these days, a sports utility vehicle.

You can just imagine the opportunities for product placement if a scene was in the kitchen. Every time they opened a cabinet or the refrigerator, there could be dozens of products seen. The product manufacturers would pay these companies a fee for getting placed in a movie or on a TV show. Some of the product placement companies have faded away, but, the ones remaining are doing quite well.

That said, we still enjoy providing product placements on TV and in

What better tie-in than a movie co-starring Buddy Hackett ("All Hands On Deck"), about a sailor and his pet turkey?

18

Contests — Always A Winner!

☆ ☆

movies, if we can work an equitable tie-in or trade-out for our clients.

As you may well know from all the cereal box-tops you collected as a child, there are all types of contests. We have been involved in every sort, with almost every client with which we've worked. We have staged recipe contests, sweepstakes, cooking contests, retail display contests, restaurant menu contests, chef cook-offs, and cooking contests at state and county fairs. Contests are a way of life in public relations and advertising.

We learned early on that contests involve two main ingredients: 1) how much money is in the budget and 2) how much time do we have to develop the contest. We also learned that to really do a contest right, one should have a "contest consultant." Yes, there actually is such a person, because each year the legal requirements get tougher and tougher. There are different city, state and federal rules pertaining to contests. In the early days, we didn't know of such things. Now, it is mandatory to know them.

For example, when we were representing Rold Gold pretzels, the client wanted to create a little excitement in Seattle, Washington, so he decided to have a contest. Very simple—or so it seemed. We would place tear-off coupon pads on the pretzel display racks, offering a television set for the best letter we received—written in the standard "25 words or less"—stating why the consumer liked Rold Gold pretzels. In those days, the prizes were black-and-white television sets. The world of television was not yet fully "in living color," as color TV was called when it began to glow in our living rooms about 1960.

A few unexpected things happened. Even though this contest was taking place only around the Seattle area, we began getting letters from all over the United States with contest entry cards enclosed. (Legally, a contestant could submit a 3"x 5" card with "Rold Gold pretzels" written on it, if he or she did not have an official entry blank.) The letters were, of course, chock full of wonderful comments about the good taste of the pretzels. Concerning most of the out-of-state responses, Rold Gold pret-

☆ ☆

zels were not even sold in those areas. What happened? Had all these people vacationed in Seattle and become pretzel fanatics while visiting? We soon found that an abundance of contest magazines and newsletters are published, telling people all over the country about contests going on anywhere and everywhere. That's why we received so many entry forms. Imagine what happens today with such contests on the Internet.

We sorted through the letters we received from the Seattle area and read the entries. Everybody in our office agreed on one particular entry as the winner; it was priceless, in advertising terms. The letter was written by a teenage girl who stated that, when she came home from school every day and asked for a snack, her mother wanted her to have the healthiest one on the market. Of course, the healthiest and best-tasting snack was Rold Gold pretzels, which she had every day with a glass of milk. What a letter! What a winner!

We sent our television set to a little town outside of Seattle, where the contestant lived. We got a phone call from her telling us the television set had arrived with a cracked screen. Not wanting to disappoint this young girl, we made arrangements for her to send the television set back, having many phone conversations with United Parcel Service to straighten out the shipping and handling problems. We decided to take a publicity photo of the winner so we could place it in grocery industry publications, in addition to the local newspaper in her area. We hadn't seen the winner in the flesh and, as she sounded like a young girl on the phone, we assumed she was at least not an alien from Mars.

We arranged with one of our associates in Seattle to take a photo of the winner with the television set and a package of Rold Gold pretzels. To our surprise, we received a call back from our friend saying, "Wait until you see the photo. Call me about your huge success when you get the picture." We called him when we received the photo; we laughed and cried over it. The winner turned out to be an elderly lady who was a professional contest entrant. (Yes, there actually are people who make a career out of entering contests.) She had written our winning letter, posing as a teenage girl. Incidentally, she did not even have a teenage girl living in the household. It taught us a lesson, even though luckily for us, it was a small contest, originally designated for a small portion of the country. We were soon to discover there are many reasons why one should hire a contest consultant—to avoid situations like this. The rules weren't as specific then as they are today; for example, many contests today require participants to be age 18 or older to enter and some require

☆ ☆

proof of residing in the United States.

The Pretzel Twist Dance Contest

Sometimes you fall into a natural promotion. A big shopping mall in the Los Angeles suburb of Pico Rivera, had a very creative promotional director. We heard the mall was planning to have a Twist Contest, complete with attending celebrities and a rock 'n roll band. The "twist" was a popular dance craze in the 1960s, which caught on like wildfire following Chubby Checker's rock 'n roll hit of the same name. The dance was easy to do; it had no partnering and no complicated steps to learn. A dancer just stood in one spot and twisted from side to side, adding all kinds of original arm movements and other acrobatics.

Since we were representing Rold Gold pretzels at the time, we realized the contest gave us a great opportunity to take advantage of the word "twist." I mean, what else does a pretzel do? We called the mall's publicity director and suggested that we have the champion Rold Gold twist dancer (a title we just created) demonstrate her winning twist dance, and we would distribute samples of Rold Gold pretzels to the audience. We had one of our pretty models, who was also a good dancer, wear a stunning bathing suit, custom-made of aluminum thread, supplied by

What a twisted tie-in—a twist dance contest and pretzels—only in America!

our client Alcoa. She appeared as "Miss Rold Gold Pretzel." We drove to the mall in a car packed full with bags of pretzels, and participated in one gigantic dance contest. Our "Miss Rold Gold Pretzel" showed everybody how to do the "Pretzel Twist," which we had created especially for the event. She moved her arms and contorted them in the shape of a pretzel while doing the standard twist dance movements.

Hundreds of teens and young adults who attended the event enjoyed the free pretzel samples and had a great time. We got some good press coverage by the local papers, and a TV news crew also showed up to shoot footage of everyone twisting with pretzels. The client was amazed at how we obtained publicity at what would ordinarily just be an excuse to hand out free samples.

You know, as an afterthought, I should have contacted Chubby Checker and asked him to write a song about the Pretzel Twist; it could have been an instant hit.

The "Miss Hot-Pants Shrimp Bar-B-Q Contest"

Then there are the contests in which participants are more involved. One of the most exciting contests we ever staged was our "Miss Hot-Pants Shrimp Bar-B-Q Contest." "Hot-pants" were the fashion rage of the early 1970s. Designers created incredible outfits for women featuring essentially very abbreviated, tight shorts. The hot-pants were accessorized with ankle-length coats; wild stockings; ornate blouses, jackets and sweaters; and sometimes even thigh-high boots. In some extremes, the hot-pants themselves might be made of silk, satin or even fur. There were even hot-pants business suits on the market, as women were entering the workplace more and more at the time. It was one of the most bizarre, and most popular, women's clothing trends ever perpetrated on the public.

Getting back to our contest. We were representing Ocean Garden Products, a major supplier of jumbo shrimp from Mexico to the United States and Japan. The company had an oversupply of shrimp that year. On behalf of our client, we were trying to convince grocery retailers that shrimp was a product which would be very exciting and popular for them to feature. We wanted to create more public awareness of the good taste and nutritional value of shrimp, so the stores could sell more.

We did not have any advertising dollars with which to place ads, so it was up to us to get all the "free" publicity we could. I was an active member of the Los Angeles Press Club, and worked with the club on many events. I contacted the club's manager and suggested having an outdoor shrimp barbecue on their patio. We served the shrimp to the press club members, which included TV, radio and newspaper reporters, photographers and editors from throughout Los Angeles. Here was an opportunity to get both pre-event and post-event publicity. That's the best kind, almost like getting a 3-for-1 deal. We could inform the public "before it happens, while it's happening and after it happened."

We sent out news releases announcing the Miss Hot-Pants Shrimp Bar-B-Q Contest and inviting participants to enter. Since we are located near Hollywood, you can imagine how many entries we received from beautiful actresses and models, who were always looking for publicity. We discovered, believe it or not, a number of them were darn good cooks.

We invited several top male television and movie stars, like Gig Young, to be judges, along with members of the Press Club. With all the good-looking actors and models in attendance, we knew we'd get great coverage by the media.

On the day the event was held, we were blessed with beautiful Southern California weather, perfect for outdoor barbecuing. We made arrangements with Big Boy Barbecues, who always liked getting publicity for their equipment, to supply us with the grills at no cost. We had other clients supply their products for the sauces and condiments, with hopes of getting them publicity, as well. Practically every television station covered the event "live" for the six o' clock news, as it took place. Since it was held in the prestigious Los Angeles Press Club, the print media also turned out in abundance to cover the story. Several radio stations also covered the activities. That night and the next day, Los Angeles saw and heard a lot about how to barbecue shrimp.

We also ended up with a bevy of beautiful models we were able to hire for some of our other future, promotional events. The contestants wore loud colors and many had designed their own outfits. It was quite a fashion statement of the time. Jackie Brett, an attractive and bright actress, won the contest. She was very promotion-minded and, for the next several months, wherever she was interviewed or photographed, she reminded the audience about our Miss Hot-Pants Shrimp Bar-B-Q Contest. Today, Jackie is a syndicated Las Vegas newspaper columnist.

The Australian Tourism Bureau gave us Paul Hogan *"tossing another shrimp on the barbie"*—these models were much better looking than Paul, and we staged it 20 years earlier!

Most importantly, we were able to draw a lot of extra attention to shrimp, increase sales for our client and have a lot of fun doing it.

A "Fair" Amount of Cooking

Vern Lanegrasse, "The Hollywood Chef"— famous culinary media personality.

The more down-to-earth contests are the cooking contests at state fairs. They are an excellent venue for getting the attention of homemakers attending the fair, because the husbands are usually over at the horse races and their kids are on the rides. Homemakers usually welcome a chance to sit down and watch the cooking contests. For several years, Lee & Associates was the main provider of contests at the Los Angeles County Fair, which is quite a big annual event that attracts people from all over Southern California. The Fair generally lasts a couple of weeks. We started with the turkey cooking contest, then went to potatoes, then chicken, then eggs and then fish and seafood. We publicized the contests through major grocery stores and food columns, inviting homemakers to come cook at the event or bring a finished product. We also held demonstrations by chefs, cooks, and home economists on the preparation of basic foods. Often, at least one radio station and one TV station would broadcast a remote show from the fair, and many of our contests would end up on the local news that day. Winning recipes would also be sent out to the media. Our friend, Vern Lanegrasse, known as "The Hollywood Chef," was often one of our presenters, and he was an excellent drawing card at the fair. He would demonstrate our clients' food

☆ ☆

products, give out samples and talk about celebrities and what he served to them at his famous parties.

The California Seafood Challenge

We also created culinary contests for chefs. For nine years, we created and produced the annual California Seafood Challenge, which was open to all professional chefs. Winners would go on to compete with chefs from other states in the major American Seafood Challenge. In the culinary industry, it was like receiving the Oscar. We asked master chefs and newspaper and magazine food writers to be judges. Contest participants were required to prepare their signature dishes under strict rules pertaining to presentation, taste, texture, cleanliness, and work habits. They were also given a "mystery box" from which they had to take several ingredients and prepare complete dishes from scratch, in a specific time period. It was very exciting and some of the chefs devised terrific recipes. For a year after that, we would promote the winning chef to the media by getting him or her on TV and radio, as well as in newspaper food sections. During this media coverage, the chef would talk about the winning recipe, the many aspects of being a top chef and, of course, talk about our client's product, fish. Our whole purpose for the client, was to instill the virtues of fish and seafood—how healthy it is and how easy it is to prepare in a variety of creative and tasty ways.

A contestant chef preparing oysters for the California Seafood Challenge.

The Dolly Madison "Juke Box" Contest

The Dolly Madison "Juke Box" Contest was another fun one. Our client, Dolly

☆ ☆

Madison, well known for their pies and cakes, had a national sweep-stakes that presented prizes to instant winners. All customers had to do was look on the inside of the Dolly Madison individual-sized fruit-pie wrapper, to determine whether they had won or not. Prizes consisted of free products and an assortment of merchandise. The grand prize was a large, commercial Wurlitzer juke box, fully loaded with records, plus a year's supply of Dolly Madison products. Just over 900,000 pies would be sold during this promotional period with only one wrapper identifying the grand prize. That's a lot of haystack to go through to find the needle.

But someone did win. A college student who had a part-time job at a local dry cleaning store in Bakersfield, California, had a daily routine. Every morning, before going to school, he would stop off at the dry cleaners and pick up garments for delivery that day on his route. The next stop he made each morning was at his neighborhood Circle K convenience store where he purchased a Dolly Madison apple pie and a small carton of milk. What a loyal customer!

One particular morning, he went into the Circle K as usual, and the store was out of apple pies. So, by the fickle lottery of fate, he bought a blueberry pie instead. On his way out of the store, he threw the pie wrapper in the waste can next to his car. He just happened to notice, out of the corner of his eye, some printing on the inside of the wrapper. Curious, he pulled the wrapper out of the trash can and read, "Congratulations! You are the Grand Prize winner. Call this phone number."

"Oh sure," he thought. "It's probably a come-on." He called the number anyway, ringing through to the Dolly Madison headquarters in Los Angeles and identified himself as the grand prize winner. He recited the code on the wrapper for verification, expecting a sales pitch or at least a "catch," but there was no gimmick. He had won the Wurlitzer juke box fair and square, over 899,999 other pie eaters.

Dolly Madison's local marketing director called our office, told Howard they had identified the grand prize winner and asked him "What do you suggest we do about it?"

Howard called the young winner and explained that he wanted to get media coverage for him and Dolly Madison. The college student was thrilled to know that he was a national winner in this contest. Howard then called a press conference at the winner's apartment and invited the media to watch the truck unload the juke box and, of course, a lot of Dolly Madison cakes and pies. Normally, this would not be that big of a media event, except for the fact that Bakersfield is a small city and almost any-

☆ ☆

thing newsworthy would garner media attention. So it was worth seizing the moment. Howard called all the local TV and radio stations and the only newspaper in town, to tell them "a Bakersfield resident had just won a national contest, against the odds of 900,000 to 1." This was quite an impressive number and it got the media all excited. Statistics work like magic.

Howard then arranged for us to meet over lunch with our prize winner and a couple of Dolly Madison executives from Los Angeles. We discussed what the winner should say to the media if anyone showed up to interview him at the press conference scheduled for that afternoon at 2 p.m. We still weren't sure whether any media would cover the event. Howard asked the Dolly Madison executives to bring lots of various products to display around the winner's apartment, in hopes of getting extra visuals during any interviews. We got to the apartment about 1:30 p.m. and set up displays of Dolly Madison pies, cakes, cupcakes and Zingers. A little bit of everything Dolly Madison baked was spread all around this tiny one-bedroom apartment, laid out on dressers, the kitchen table, on top of the television set, anywhere and everywhere they could be placed. It is a good thing for us the winner was such a faithful customer. He allowed us to redecorate his apartment with wall-to-wall goodies.

Howard met the Wurlitzer delivery truck in front of the apartment building and instructed the drivers to wait a few blocks away and come back about 2:05 p.m., hopefully to make a dramatic entrance. To our delight and relief, between 2 p.m. and 2:05 p.m., media began to arrive right on cue. A few actually showed up just as the truck pulled in front to begin unloading the juke box, the dramatic moment. Reporters from the Bakersfield newspaper, two radio stations, and three TV stations—virtually all the media in town—ran toward the truck. They literally reported everything from the moment the truck drivers lowered the juke box and wheeled it into the apartment, to the pleasure and glee of the young student. Fortunately, the apartment was on the ground floor, because the juke box was huge; it filled up a good portion of his tiny living room.

The event became a total frenzy. One would have thought the President of the United States had made a surprise visit, considering all the media that showed up. I saw all those microphones stuck in this overwhelmed college kid's face, with reporters asking him what it felt like to be the "one in 900,000 winner" and did he like fruit pies? *Did he like fruit pies?* Only for breakfast every day! He proceeded to tell the story of how he had retrieved the winning wrapper as an afterthought. We even had him eating a Dolly Madison fruit pie during the interview. I might add that, since he loved them anyway, he ate it with the gusto that only a college kid can give to food. I have often imagined him becoming the proverbial BMOC (Big Man On Campus), with that juke box and all those records, not to mention a year's supply of Dolly Madison goodies; he could throw great parties from then on.

When the press conference was over, we offered Dolly Madison products to all the media, who were very appreciative and thanked us. They left almost as quickly as they came, to go on to whatever other big story of the day might be waiting for them. We hired a monitoring service to check all of the TV news shows that night, as well as the radio shows. We also alerted our news clipping service to monitor the newspaper.

A few days later, when we heard from all our monitoring sources, we were very pleased to get radio tapes, TV tapes, and of course, a clipping from the Bakersfield Californian newspaper. This was such a big news story for this small town that the TV stations used close-ups of the Dolly Madison products to tease the six and eleven o'clock news viewers, as the lead story that night—"Local Bakersfield Resident Wins National Contest."

We were confident the sales of Dolly Madison fruit pies went up considerably over the next few weeks, at least in Bakersfield. You might even say we were as "pleased as apple pie."

19

Hollywood Public Relations — Then and Now

☆ ☆

Looking back over my career in advertising and public relations from my perspective, I see there's more of everything today than 50 years ago. We have more people, more products, more media outlets, more retailers and more opportunities. This means more people are vying for media exposure. Public relations professionals are still the messengers to the media, and the media are the messengers to the public. Like many of us, people who work in the media never have enough hours in the day to get all their work done. They are under unrelenting pressure from their bosses, pressure to produce more attention-grabbing stories to get higher ratings or readership. Therefore, those of us who are communicating with them have to move fast—faster than we ever did before; and we have to be even more creative.

Obviously, communication has sped up incredibly with the implementation of cell phones, fax machines, voice-mail and the Internet, all of which did not become standard tools until the 1990s. These innovations make it easier to reach more media outlets. The flip side being that more companies are looking for media exposure than before because there exists many more goods and services. We can choose to view that solely in competitive terms, or we can see it as the dawn of undreamed possibilities in human contact and expansion. This expanded global communication is our next great frontier.

We must join the clutter and see what we can do to have our messages stand out to be seen or heard. Obviously, in writing news releases, we still have to stick with the old "who, what, when, where, why and how" formula. News writing has to be kept short and sweet; the media refuse to be cluttered with a lot of data. They want just the basic information—nothing more. If they're interested, they will let you know.

Publicity and public relations of yesteryear seem to be generally thought of mostly as gimmicky promotions and stunts created by overzealous press agents. Their presumed goal was to attract any kind of attention to their client, even if it was silly; rather than to allow the public to become legitimately educated about their clients.

☆ ☆

Traditional gimmicks are still as good today

All the movie studios, for example, hired press agents to create an event or any activity to get press coverage for the release of a new movie or draw attention to its stars. Who do you think called all the photographers, now commonly referred to as the paparazzi, to tip them that Marilyn Monroe or Frank Sinatra was dining at a certain restaurant? You still see it today. Tom Cruise or Barbra Streissand step out of a restaurant and hundreds of blinding flashes go off as photographers shoot away. Who alerted the media? The celebrity's agent? Or perhaps a publicity person representing the restaurant?

Some gimmicks or promotions are just as good today as they were many years ago and they still result in media coverage to different degrees, from local to national or even international. Consider the local County Fair beauty queen. She is certainly a good reason for a reporter and a photographer to show up on opening day. They can put her picture in the local paper to draw attention to when the fair opens and where it is held, what kinds of activities will be taking place, and so on.

I'm sure you are all familiar with the annual Pasadena Tournament of Roses Parade, televised every New Year's Day, preceding the Rose Bowl, one of the most popular college football championship games. The "Rose Parade" has been going strong for well over a century. The colorful floats represent a wide variety of corporations that want their 30 seconds of glory to promote their product or service by getting mentioned and having their logo seen by many of millions of people around the world.

Press photographers and the "papparazzi"
have been around almost as long as the camera.

There will always be other attention-grabbing publicity stunts, such as the world's biggest Bloody Mary, a co-op promotional project consisting of 12 gallons of Tabasco® Brand Pepper Sauce, 815 gallons of V8® 100% Vegetable Juice and 204 gallons of Finlandia® Vodka, garnished with 15,000 stalks of celery. The Millennium Mary™ was presented in a 10-foot-tall glass, in the heart of the world-renown French Quarter in New Orleans to welcome revelers into the new Millennium on New Year's Day in the year 2000.

Actually, more traditional public relations, used mainly to disseminate valuable and/or new information to persuade or gain favorable impressions toward a company, product or service, has become more important than ever, to help get the message out to a targeted public. This is especially true as our population continues to grow and society continues to become more segmented, as well. Public relations activities must become even more targeted to specific groups for maximum effectiveness.

Ushering in the new Millennium with the world's largest Bloody Mary cocktail.

Celebrities and Charities

In the early days of my career, I recall that celebrities worked hard. They got up very early in the morning for makeup, then put in a full day's work. Somehow, they still had plenty of time on weekends, and between movie assignments, to attend many celebrity events. They participated in such activities as playing in celebrity tennis matches, golf tournaments or appearing on various celebrity telethons to raise money for worthwhile charities.

Many also attended glitzy Hollywood movie premieres, just to make an appearance. Today, celebrities are under much more pressure. Their agents have many things scheduled for them, and almost everything has gone to the money aspect.

Certainly, I know of many well established, or young, up and coming celebrities, who volunteer their name and their time to worthy causes. In many cases, if you are not doing a major, promotional, cross-merchandising tie-in—something with your client's product and a film studio's latest movie, involving a premium giveaway at a fast food restaurant—or working with a major charity that has a close, personal meaning to a star—chances are you will not have much access to a big-name celebrity.

Sometimes, I could not believe how lucky I was to get the cooperation of such huge movie and TV stars to work with me to help publicize my clients' products, from Abbott & Costello promoting eggs, to Groucho promoting potatoes, and for no money—just lots of work on our part. These types of promotions can still happen today, but not as often. Usually, there would have to be a huge benefit to the celebrity to get her or him involved. There are exceptions, and to be fair, I want to point out a "from the heart" example: ultra-famous

Seven-time 1972 Olympic gold medalist, Mark Spitz, enjoying a moment with our "Miss Good Egg" (Karen Lindsey) during a mid '70s Jerry Lewis telethon.

international superstar Arnold Schwartz-enegger, dressed as Santa Claus, generously donated his valuable time to hand out Christmas gifts to disadvantaged children at Hollenbeck Youth Center in East Los Angeles. Lee & Associates usually donates food and beverages garnered from our clients for the many hard-working volunteers at various charity functions. This time, we also provided hundreds of toy Panda bears donated by our client, Panda Express (America's largest Chinese fast-food restaurant chain), for Arnold to distribute.

Arnold Schwartzenegger distributes stuffed toy Pandas to children in East Los Angeles.

In the mid-20th century, celebrities did not have as many outlets to promote themselves, their movies, or their TV shows as they do today. We provided an excellent opportunity for them to reach a different type of audience, other than just the standard "Hollywood" media, such as the Hollywood Reporter, Variety, or the movie columns in newspapers and magazines. The fact that we were able to get them major publicity in the food sections of newspapers and magazines nationwide was a novelty for them. By posing with our clients' food products, celebrities were able to reach entire families who were not only viewers of their films or TV shows, but they were potential customers of these products, as well. They could often be photographed in a wholesome, family setting and were thrilled to cooperate.

☆ ☆

Today, the celebrity's time is limited and their agents are considering what will bring in the big bucks for what used to be reciprocity in publicity; "You do something for me and I'll do something for you."

Too Much News

These days, I have noticed that the media are overburdened with messages whereas, in the past, they were often hungry for story ideas. Unfortunately, because there are more media outlets, news programs and other sources, including more cable television channels being continually added, the media are under terrible pressure to outdo each other for ratings, more than ever. To our chagrin, the "shock-value stories," such as the thrilling car chases and mass murders, are repeated over and over again on TV. Soft features, good news, and general interest news is lost because of the rush to get the audience. However, since a PR person has many more media outlets today that were not available in the past, the odds of getting media exposure may actually be greater.

The challenge in the past was to be creative and newsworthy enough to get extra media exposure. On TV, we could get a reasonable amount of airtime for product exposure, from several minutes to even a half-hour on some shows. We're not able to get as long an exposure for our clients' products on the typical talk shows that are on now, compared to the tremendous segments I got on many Steve Allen and Dinah Shore shows.

Today, most news is clutter, reported in 10-second to 30-second "headline" news bytes. For example, before a recent Thanksgiving we were promoting turkeys, stuffing, and other holiday foods. We had one of our registered dietitian consultants, talented Nancy Berkoff, who is also a chef and an instructor at a culinary college, appear on several radio and television shows. At one particular TV station, we arranged for her to appear in a taped segment on a morning news program and, in only four minutes, Nancy presented food safety hints and interesting tips on how to make a complete turkey dinner that was quick and easy to prepare. It was very educational, highly visual, and a fabulous presentation the average homemaker would appreciate, especially before the Thanksgiving holiday. But the producer of that segment wanted to edit it down to 60 seconds! The final edit actually came to about 90 seconds, which was barely enough time to whiz a few ideas past the viewing consumer. Still, I was happy to have our clients' products be seen on a top TV news show for some positive exposure, even if it was for less time. Nancy was a real pro and handled everything smoothly and professionally. In spite of today's time constraints, through her efforts, we ended up with a tight, yet informative, holiday show.

Food Publicity

When I began producing food publicity in the 1950s—and for many years thereafter—not many food publicists were around. Meticulous in my research, I utilized home economists, chefs, dietitians, and food technologists. I spent a great deal of time being very academic about testing recipes and being concerned with health and food safety, calories, nutrition, and so on. As the field grew, more food manufacturers noticed the need for publicity. Therefore, as the years went on, more PR professionals were increasingly tasked to publicize their various clients' products. There became a clutter because the media was overwhelmed and couldn't possibly use everybody's material all the time. That's why, by my being able to work with celebrities, associated with my clients' products, I was able to get unconventional, positive publicity exposure, before all the clutter even began. I was always happy to be able to contribute my style of PR creativity in helping to develop the "food public relations" category. Now, there are many more agencies also specializing in food promotion, as well as in a variety of areas in public relations that did not exist many years ago. These PR specialties include health, financial, charity, sports, entertainment, business-to-business and high-tech, among others.

Chef/Dietician and client spokesperson, Nancy Berkoff, in a typical TV show setup, discussing holiday cooking tips with "Weekend" show host Raff Ahlgren in San Diego, California.

Greer Garson posing with our client's product to show how earlier Hollywood entertaining could be a glamorous affair.

☆ ☆

A New Hollywood

I was recently discussing the "then and now" of Hollywood public relations with two of my long-time friends and PR colleagues, Irwin Zucker and Julian Myers. Irwin was in the record promotion business for many years and is now one of the top book publicists in the country. Julian's area of public relations expertise is in the entertainment industry, having promoted some of the biggest stars in Hollywood. He has also taught an extension course at UCLA for over 20 years called "Entertainment PR." They both agree with me that things are moving faster than ever in every facet of business, especially in public relations.

"Obviously, the consumers are bombarded with messages, services and products to buy," says Irwin. "So, those of us who are giving out the messages have to fight for more attention, whether we are promoting a movie, a new book, a packaged product, a grocery item, or anything."

He adds, "Today, knowing how best to utilize the Internet is another avenue to disseminate messages. It is a great benefit to publicists, both in terms of research and in making new contacts. No one, as yet, can even calculate the potential audiences that can be reached. But there's still no substitute for good, traditional print, TV and radio interviews to obtain a tremendous amount of publicity."

Leo setting up a publicity photo of Barbara Eden and eggs.

☆ ☆

Before he began his successful business of promoting celebrities, Julian began his career in the entertainment business with creative responsibilities at such film industry giants as Columbia Pictures, MGM, and 20th Century Fox. He says that with the proper special event effort and the right celebrity, the media are more likely to give lots of coverage. He adds, "Promotional tie-ins with movies and products are now generally on a big scale. Many millions of dollars are invested in almost every promotion that gets created. Just think of a new movie coming out, especially one that appeals to kids, and you will think of McDonald's or Burger King giving away toys that relate to the movie. Or, for adults, think of James Bond and you will think of a sporty BMW."

Irwin and Julian both tell me that there are more celebrities today than many years ago. There are more movies and more TV shows being made today, due in part to the speed in editing and even animation, thanks to all of the new technology in the film and TV industries. This allows for more characters to be created, and thus, more actors, resulting in more celebrities. The phenomenon of "escalating celebs" has encouraged a growth industry of celebrity award shows. In addition to TV's Emmy Awards and the motion picture industry's Academy Awards, there's the Golden Globe Awards, the People's Choice Awards, TV Guide Awards and several other popular award shows. People just love celebrities.

"Not Enough Hours"

"Nothing valuable is ever lost by taking time." Abraham Lincoln said that 150 years ago. I wonder if he would feel the same way today. In our society of the new millennium, we are driven to accomplish more than we have hours in the day to do it. Is this a good thing, or is something valuable being lost?

I don't want to generalize, but I think personal contact is a missing ingredient, the "something valuable" Abraham Lincoln referred to in his famous quote. I think a perfect example of this trend in our society is an AT&T television commercial showing a mother and her two children. One of her kids says to her, "Mom, let's go the beach." The mother replies, "I can't, I have a client meeting." The little girl responds by asking, "Mom, can I be a client?" There's a pause, and the mother says with a smile, cell phone in hand, "Let's go to the beach." I think that tells the whole story.

It is my sincere hope that this trend toward "no time" will reverse itself. It is questionable to me whether we are really accomplishing more or, in actuality, losing the valued relationships we took for granted for so long.

On the other hand, finding a way to streamline all the clutter and create a more normal pace could catapult society into a golden age over the next millennium. Maybe we just have not, as yet, figured out the most expedient use for these wildly advanced technologies that are so far beyond what any of us could imagine in the past. The Internet has opened up exciting new vistas, allowing for all of us to grow and work with each other, and to understand one another better. Cultures are better able to share ideas, philosophies, fashions and most certainly, foods. In the face of all that, the essential key for all of us, is to remain true to our basic honesty and a high, ethical standard.

Fifty years ago, the prognosticators were saying that by now, machines would have taken over to the point that all our time would be spent in leisure and pursuing creative interests. Somehow we've missed the boat on that one! But it is still a goal worth considering.

20

Shooting For The Stars

☆ ☆

I have fond memories of working with many of the biggest names in Hollywood, as well as famous athletes. I noticed an interesting characteristic: for the most part, the bigger the star, the nicer they are.

Photos are an extremely important part of just about any successful publicity campaign. The old adage is true: "A picture is worth a thousand words." Every photo tells a different story. I have tons of photos; that's why I always have a story or two to tell about a celebrity. I feel privileged to have been allowed into many celebrities' homes or on the sets of movie and TV studios, to arrange photos of these stars posing with my clients' products.

You can't get any bigger in show business than Bob Hope, and he was one of the nicest stars of all. As busy as he was, we were fortunate to have the opportunity to participate in reciprocal publicity promotions with him. His publicity agent, Frank Lieberman, helped us arrange photos of Bob to promote our Coachella Valley grapefruit industry client with his huge, celebrity golf tournament charity, each year.

Frank also represented Phyllis Diller. After he introduced us, she

The always lovely Miss Diller
demonstrating her gourmet cooking abilities, preparing "fish roll-ups."

Phyllis Diller accepting her "Corniest Comedienne" basket of corn award from Howard Pearlstein.

invited us into her home on several occasions to photograph her cooking with many of our clients' products, including corn, seafood, Mrs. Cubbison's Dressing Mix and prunes. She's very talented in the kitchen, as well as on stage; relatively few people know Phyllis is actually a gourmet cook with a cookbook to her credit.

In addition to getting Phyllis publicity in the food sections of newspapers around the country, which also promoted our clients' products, we created an award for her on behalf of our California corn industry client. It proclaimed her the "Corniest Comedienne" and we used that as another opportunity to leverage more publicity for both Phyllis and our client.

Another talented celebrity gourmet cook was Vincent Price, famous for his scary roles in many horror films. Who would have thought when he would "scare something up in the kitchen," that it would actually be innovative and tasty? Vincent and his wife, Mary, developed a series of cookbooks, as well as a packaged set of audiocassettes with Vincent's distinctive and provocative voice narrating how the listener could create his delicious, gourmet recipes.

Vincent Price and one of our home economists, Martha Kimball, cooking up a new prune recipe.

Since he included some of my clients' products in his recipes, such as prunes and

Armanino chopped chives, I would help promote his books and tapes by having photos made of him while cooking or posing with completed meals he prepared. I also arranged for him to be interviewed on certain TV and radio shows. His book of connoisseurs' recipes, called *"Treasury of Great Recipes,"* included truly wonderful dishes. It's comforting to know that someone who could be so frightening on the big screen was actually a kind gentleman in a big kitchen. Having the opportunity to visit with him several times during photo sessions or after a TV or radio interview, was a memorable experience for me, and not scary at all.

I always enjoyed working with Dinah Shore and Steve Allen, creating some of the wildest, funniest, and yet informative, segments on their variety TV shows that you can imagine. Our reward was getting great exposure for my clients' products on dozens of prime time TV shows. Just seeing some of the still photos from these shows makes you realize the real star power they had, from Rock Hudson and Angie Dickinson to Jimmy Stewart and Lucille Ball. You can see in the photos there was a lot of interaction with our clients' products. I still laugh every time I see a tape of Steve in some of the crazy set-ups we put together for him.

Arranging publicity photos to accompany stories, and many times getting a variety of recipes to highlight a wide range of food products, often brought us in contact with an interesting array of celebrities. Work-

(l. to r.) "Omelet King" Howard Helmer shows Angie Dickenson, Dinah Shore and Rock Hudson how simple omelet making can be—even blindfolded!

ing with famous athletes was occasionally an enjoyable surprise. We never knew what to expect. When football legend Roosevelt "Rosie" Grier came to our office, he was part of a celebrity cooking event tie-in with a charity fundraiser. He gave us a recipe featuring artichokes. Since we represented the California Artichoke Advisory Board, we invited him into our kitchen to shoot photos of him preparing his dish.

We pictured this physically huge mean-looking former football player as a person who would probably be in a hurry and uncooperative. When he arrived at our office, Rosie, who just barely made it through the doorway because he's so large, towered over everyone. While visiting with him for a few moments, I learned that this surprisingly gentle man enjoyed cooking, and proudly informed me that he was also quite good at his new hobby of doing needlepoint. Can you imagine a great pro football player needlepointing, and admitting it?

He was a delight to work with and we got great photos to send to food editors all over the country to help promote the charity and artichokes. I understand, these days the retired football star is in the ministry and works to help disadvantaged children. I often think of him as the gentle giant who likes to cook and needlepoint.

Rosie Grier,
"Gentleman Giant."

☆ ☆

Another famous athlete I worked with on publicity photos was a young George Foreman, who had just become World Heavyweight Boxing Champion in 1973. (Something quite remarkable about George is, after losing his title to Muhammad Ali in 1974, he came back 20 years later to recapture his title from Michael Moorer in 1994, at the age of 45, making him the oldest man to win the heavyweight boxing crown.)

I arranged for my favorite spokesmodel, Karen Lindsey, who was "Miss Golden Egg," to present George with a "good egg" award, on behalf of the California egg industry. It was to congratulate him for winning his prestigious boxing title.

We always knew George was a good egg.

I discovered George was going to be at the Frontier Hotel in Las Vegas. Since we were sending Karen there as part of a multi-city media tour to promote eggs, we arranged her schedule so she would be in Las Vegas at the same time as George. Between all of his press conferences and Karen's TV and radio interviews, we somehow managed to get the two of them together for some publicity photos.

George was just as nice as could be and still a little dazed over being the new heavyweight champion. He was very courteous and accommodating to us. This celebrity status was all new to him. When the photos and a news release were sent out with some tasty egg recipes, we received a tremendous amount of publicity promoting the healthy qualities of eggs. After all, we had the most famous athlete in the world in a photo with Miss Golden Egg. What more could a publicist ask for?

Because we worked for the turkey industry, and Mrs. Cubbison's Dressing Mix, over the years, we took many photos with celebrities that featured Thanksgiving and Christmas themes. Some of my favorite photos are the family shots we arranged with celebrities like Lloyd Bridges with his wife, Dorothy, daughter Cindy, and two young sons, Beau and Jeff. Who would have thought both his sons would grow up to be big stars like their dad? When I phoned Lloyd, just a few months before his untimely death, to tell him I was gathering lots of old photos for this book and found some photos of him and his kids, he was very happy to learn of my discovery. He said he remembered posing for the photos but didn't recall seeing them and asked me to send him copies. He couldn't wait to see his grownup children as kids again.

Some "TV families" we posed with a holiday theme—except they were on a sound stage instead of in a real home—include the casts of "The Danny Thomas Show," "The Real McCoys," "My Three Sons" and "Lassie." My own three boys got a real kick out of the fact that their dad actually met these TV families, because those fictitious families seemed so real to them when they were young. They watched all of these shows,

*Lloyd Bridges giving a few carving tips to his family
at holiday time with not-yet-famous sons, Beau (l.), and Jeff (r.) in attendance.*

☆ ☆

The "Lassie" TV family (l. to r.) Hugh Reilly, June Lockhart and Jon Provost, being presented a holiday turkey by Gene Beals, manager of the California Turkey Advisory Board.

On the set of "My Three Sons," with (l. to r.) William Frawley, Tim Considine, Fred MacMurray, Don Grady, and Stanley Livingston.

The cast members of "The Danny Thomas Show," made room for turkey (l. to r.)
Angela Cartwright, Marjorie Lord, Danny Thomas, Sherry Jackson and Rusty Hamer.

"The Real McCoys" (l. to r., Richard Crenna, Kathleen Nolan,
Walter Brennan, Tony Martinez) knew the real McCoy when they tasted it!

☆ ☆

as did almost every kid in America.

Bing Crosby was very generous with his time, allowing us to photograph him for Thanksgiving on the set of his weekly TV show. These photos helped us get publicity for the turkey industry, while he received added exposure for his show. Photos of other singers you'll see in this book, posed with our clients' products, range from Wayne Newton and Glen Campbell to Tennessee Ernie Ford, Pat Boone, Rita Moreno and Liberace, to name a few. We covered the whole vocal range of singers.

Bing Crosby in Pilgrim regalia, hamming it up for turkey day.

Leo presenting Liberace's holiday turkey beside his piano-shaped swimming pool.

☆ ☆

"Golden Throat" meets "Golden Egg"—Wayne Newton and Miss Golden Egg, Karen Lindsey.

Tennessee Ernie Ford and his power tools.

☆ ☆ ☆ ☆ ☆ ☆ ☆ ☆ ☆ ☆ ☆ ☆ ☆ ☆ ☆ ☆ ☆ ☆ ☆

*Pat Boone and a fine
feathered friend.*

*Rita Moreno always looking great—
even when serving friends at her
turkey barbecue.*

*Glen Campbell talking
up the nutritional value
of prunes.*

☆ ☆

A couple of years ago, prior to Thanksgiving we asked some of our talent agent friends if they handled any celebrities who were not only big stars, but were also good cooks. We wanted to set up a series of holiday-themed photos with a celebrity in the kitchen. One of them mentioned that his newest client was Mickey Rooney. He told us that Mickey was about to appear on Broadway in a new stage production of The Wizard of Oz, and was coming out in a sequel to the popular movie "Babe," called "Pig In The City" and would like to get some publicity on his projects.

I thought, Mickey Rooney? Available to me to be photographed with some of my clients' products just before Thanksgiving, at no cost? I immediately replied, "I'm sure I can think of a way to work Mickey in."

No question, Mickey Rooney is one of the most famous stars of our time. With over 100 movie, television and theater credits, as well as Oscar and Emmy recognitions, who would have thought he could add the talent of being a pretty good cook to his accomplishments, as well? I remember enjoying his performances in many films including "A Midsummer Night's Dream," "National Velvet," several Andy Hardy movies, "The Black Stallion," and scores of appearances on dramatic, comedy and variety TV shows. His fine career actually goes back into the silent film era in the original "Our Gang" comedies.

I met with my sons, Howard and Frank, and asked how they were coming along on the holiday promotion for our Mrs. Cubbison's account and where we could use Mickey Rooney. They immediately thought of arranging for him to do TV and radio interviews to talk about how much he likes to cook. Then he could offer Thanksgiving preparation tips and serving suggestions, including Mrs. Cubbison's as an ingredient.

After learning of Mickey's incredibly busy schedule over the next two months, there was no time to do much more than squeeze in a photo session during the next week. We could then release photos of Mickey preparing and cooking a turkey with dressing and all the trimmings, just in time for Thanksgiving. The release would mention Mickey's current activities.

He was nice enough to come to our office and meet with us to discuss the project. He was extremely cordial and was joking around with us, yet was serious when discussing what we felt would be appropriate arrangements for the photo session. The most practical setup would be to have Mickey show up at an appointed time at a convenient location in Beverly Hills with everything prepared and ready to use. We would pose him in the kitchen with the food and have one of our photographers start shooting away. Mickey shared his favorite turkey dressing recipe with us ahead of time; it was quite creative and very tasty (see recipe Chapter 22).

Not wanting to leave anything to chance, we brought in both a home economist and a food stylist to cook the turkey and dressing, and to set up the counter area and the entire kitchen, so everything would look perfect in the photo.

He arrived right on time at 10:30 am. The photographer had been there since 8:00 am setting up his lights and checking out the best angles for the photos. The home economist and food stylist also arrived a couple of hours earlier, to get everything set up for the food and background setting. We had two turkeys, one uncooked for the preparation shots, and one cooked, with all the trimmings, for the finished, beauty shots. We also had plenty of Mrs. Cubbison's dressing on hand to stuff the turkeys and to make into casseroles.

Before Howard, who was coordinating the activities, even had a chance to say "hello" to Mickey and introduce him to the photographer and go over the sequence of shots, something happened that was both funny and horrifying, from a production point of view. Mickey picked up the huge carving knife and while he was still saying "hello" to everyone, he grabbed the leg of the finished turkey and started to carve it. That was supposed to

*Howard sets up
the photo shoot with Mickey.*

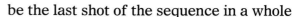

Who knew Mickey Rooney is a leg man?

Mickey poses for a good "action" shot of preparing turkey dressing.

be the last shot of the sequence in a whole series of shots. He thought we were going to take only action shots of him in the kitchen. So, he gave us plenty of action.

Fortunately, the turkey was already stuffed and there was a finished, cooked casserole of dressing right next to it. The photographer started shooting away while Mickey hammed it up for the camera and proceeded to entertain everyone in the room, doing his impression of a doctor performing surgery—on the turkey—even the outakes were funny.

We were never able to take a final "beauty shot" of the finished, stuffed turkey, since one of its legs had been cut off. But we did get plenty of good photos for publicity, just in time for Thanksgiving. Whenever I see one of those photos, I think to myself, "Who would ever have thought I would be with one of Hollywood's greatest legends—stuffing a turkey?"

In addition to the many vintage celebrity photos that you have seen throughout this book, the following pages contain a collection of many photos of my favorite celebrities, shot for the countless product promotion campaigns that I have worked on with Hollywood royalty over the last 50 years. I'm sure that you will enjoy seeing and rediscovering many famous stars, as I have, while compiling this book.

21

Celebrity Photo Gallery

☆ ☆

The following pages show examples of a variety of our promotional activities with celebrities over the last 50 years. These include presenting them with awards of appreciation for posing with our clients' products to draw attention to their nutritional value, such as plaques from the California Dairy Council or the Golden Egg Award; publicity photos of celebrities with our clients' products in their own kitchens or that were served at a special event; and also visiting with celebrities at various charity events to talk about possible promotional tie-ins with their upcoming TV show, movie, record album or other big event.

Leo, Bill Cosby

Leo, Tony Curtis, Janet Leigh

Phyllis Diller

Leo, Vincent Price

George Burns and Gracie Allen

Mohammad Ali, Leo

Howard Pearlstein, Joe Theisman, Frank Pearlstein

Laurence Welk

Valerie Perrine

Howard Pearlstein, Ed McMahon

Ron Masak, Joy Mahaffey

☆ ☆

Leo, Carroll O'Connor

Joseph Campanella

Tim Reid, Snoopy

Jimmy Durante and dancer, Jeanne Carroll

Buddy Hackett

Jo Ann Pflug

Glenn Ford

Leo, Frank Sinatra, Jr.   *Terry Moore*   *Roger Smith, Leo*

Leo, Juliet Mills   *Vera Ellen*   *Danish Cheese Girl,*
Sugar Ray Robinson

Leo, Rafer Johnson   *Howard Pearlstein, Richard Deacon*

☆ ☆

Robert and Flora Alda

Snoopy, Harvey Korman

Tom Hatten

Frank Pearlstein, Dave Winfield

Elinor Donahue

John Davidson

Danish Cheese Girl, Howard Duff

☆ ☆ ☆ ☆ ☆ ☆ ☆ ☆ ☆ ☆ ☆ ☆ ☆ ☆ ☆ ☆ ☆ ☆ ☆ ☆

Edgar Bergen, Jack Benny, Frances Bergen, Leo   *Johnny Mathis and the Grapefruit Girls*

L.A. Mayor Bradley with various "Misses"   *Julia Meade*

Linda Crystal, Leif Ericson   *Rip Taylor*

22

Recipes Of The Stars

The following pages feature a small, representative sample of our many celebrity recipes that have been released over the years. Many of them appeared in our Western Research Kitchens "Recipe of the Week" feature in the *T.V. Fanfare* weekly publication, distributed in supermarkets throughout the country.

Here's to good food—good cooking—and good eating!

Bill Cosby's
PRUNE-NUT DRESSING

2 6-oz. bags of seasoned dressing
1 cup butter
2 cups chopped prunes
2 cups chopped pecans
1½ cups prune juice
10-14 whole prunes
10-14 whole pecans

Combine dressing with butter, chopped prunes and pecans. Add liquid gradually. Mix ingredients. Place dressing in lightly greased 2-qt. casserole dish, packing down lightly. Stuff each whole prune with a pecan half. Top with stuffed prunes and cover casserole with aluminum foil; press to seal. Bake at 325°F for 45 min. or until done. Yields 8 to 10 servings.

Ronnie Schell's
"BREAKFAST IN A BLENDER"

6 oz. cranberry juice
2 tbsp. oat bran
2 tbsp. wheat bran
1 tbsp. brewer's yeast
½ cup blueberries*
1 cup strawberries*
1 cup sliced or cubed mango*
  or papaya*
1 banana
1 tbsp. peanut butter
2 tbsp. whey protein powder
½ tsp. vitamin C crystals

*Fresh or frozen

Blend until the consistency of a thick milk shake. Serve with a small bowl of pitted prunes. Yields 4 (6-oz.) servings.

Mickey Rooney's
KAHLUA SAVORY DRESSING

8 oz. pork or turkey
sausage
½ cup pecans, toasted
and chopped
1 cup celery, diced
1 cup onions, diced
1 cup raisins

2 6-oz. bags Mrs. Cubbison's
Seasoned Dressing
2 tbsp. parsley, minced
2 tsp. grated orange zest
⅓ cup Kahlua
1 14 oz. can chicken broth

In a large skillet, cook sausage, breaking up the meat for about
three minutes until browned. Remove from skillet and drain off
drippings.
Toast pecans by placing in a dry skillet on medium heat. Stir
pecans in skillet for five minutes. Remove and cool. Chop pecans.
Mix remaining ingredients together in a large bowl. Let stand to
assure dressing is moistened by the liquid.
Cool thoroughly before stuffing the turkey. Wrap extra dressing
in foil, or place in a casserole dish to roast with the turkey the
last 30 minutes of cooking. With the addition of a beaten egg, the
mixture can be wrapped in foil, rolled into the shape of a long tube
(twist ends closed) and baked 45 min. at 350°F. Slice into small,
round portions.
Yields 8 half-cup servings (three qts. dressing; enough for a 12
to 14-lb. turkey).

Phyllis Diller's
BAKED DILL-STUFFED SOLE

3 lbs. fillet of sole or halibut
1 6-oz. bag Mrs. Cubbison's
Cornbread Stuffin'
¼ cup melted butter
¼ cup chopped dill pickles
¼ cup minced onion
1 egg, beaten

2 tbsp. or less dry
white wine
1 onion, sliced very thin
1 tomato, sliced very thin
Salt, pepper and sweet
basil, to taste

Butter a shallow baking dish and place half the fish in it. Make
stuffing by combining and mixing the cornbread stuffin', melted
butter, dill pickle, minced onion if desired, salt and pepper, beaten
egg and enough wine to moisten to your desired consistency.
Spread the stuffing over the fish in the baking dish. Top with
remaining fish. On top of fish, arrange thin onion slices, then tomato
slices. Sprinkle with salt and pepper and sweet basil to taste. Bake
about 40 minutes at 350°F or until fish flakes with a fork.
Yields 6-8 servings.

Jack La Lanne's
GRAVENSTEIN APPLE PIE

5-7 Gravenstein (or other baking) apples
¾-1 cup honey
2 tbsp. whole wheat pastry flour
⅛ tsp. salt
1 tsp. cinnamon
¼ tsp. nutmeg

Pare apples and slice thin. Add honey and mix with whole wheat flour, salt and spices. Fill 9-inch pastry-lined pan. Brush pastry with vegetable oil. Adjust top crust. Bake in hot oven 10 min. at 450°F, then in moderate oven, about 40 min. at 350°F. If apples are not tart enough, add 1 tablespoon lemon juice or grated lemon peel.
Yields 10-12 servings.

Francine York's
FILLET A LA PECHE

1 lb. cod or sole fillets
½ cup cond. skimmed milk
¼ cup canned sliced mushrooms
1½ tsp. seasoned salt
Dash of pepper
⅛ tsp. thyme
⅛ tsp. tarragon leaves

1 bay leaf
¼ cup breadcrumbs
2 tsp. melted butter
6-8 cling peach slices
2 tsp. chopped chives
Dash of paprika

Place fish fillets in shallow baking pan. Cover with milk, mushrooms and seasonings. Bake in preheated oven for 8 minutes at 375°F or until almost done. Meanwhile, mix together breadcrumbs and melted butter. Sprinkle over fillets. Arrange peach slices on top. Sprinkle with chopped chives and a dash of paprika. Bake 2 to 3 min. longer, or until fish flakes with a fork.
Yields 4 servings.

Bob Hope's
HONEYED-FIG GRAPEFRUIT HALVES

6 dried figs
¼ cup honey
¼ cup water
3 grapefruit, cut into halves

Combine dried figs, honey and water in saucepan for sauce. Cover and simmer for 10 min. Cool. Cut around membranes of grapefruit to loosen, using a sharp, paring knife. Cut each fig into 5 or 6 slices. Arrange one sliced fig on each half grapefruit. Spoon syrup over top. Garnish plate with extra figs, if desired.
Yields 6 servings.

Western Research Kitchens'
CHIVE HANGTOWN FRY

12 oysters
¼ cup butter or margarine
6 eggs
¼ cup light cream
¼ cup chopped chives
Salt and pepper

Shuck oysters and sauté in butter until edges curl. Beat eggs and cream together. Pour mixture over oysters. Sprinkle with chives. Cook over low heat, stirring constantly until mixture is scrambled, but still moist. Season to taste with salt and pepper. Serve with a crisp salad and slice of hot toast.
Yields 6 servings.

☆ ☆ ☆

Frank Sinatra Jr.'s
SAUTÉED ZUCCHINI

1 clove garlic, chopped
2 tbsp. olive oil
8 small zucchinis, unpeeled,
   cut into julienne sticks
½ tsp. dried parsley
½ tsp. dried basil
Salt and pepper, to taste
4 tbsp. grated Parmesan
   or Romano cheese

Sauté garlic in olive oil until brown, remove and discard. Add zucchini and sauté. Add parsley and basil. Stir zucchini until the herbs have distributed throughout. Add salt and pepper to taste. Top with about a tablespoon of cheese per serving.
Yields 4 servings.

☆ ☆ ☆

Dinah Shore's
PRUNE WHIP & PORT WINE

½ lb. pitted prunes
⅔ cup granulated sugar
3 lemon slices, with rind
1 cup port wine
1 cup whipping cream
1 tbsp. confectioner's
   sugar
Almonds, blanched,
   slivered and toasted

Place prunes, sugar and lemon slices in a saucepan. Cover with water and bring to a boil. Simmer for 5 min. Drain (save the juice). Leave prunes in pan and add most of the wine and cook 10 min. longer. Puree the prunes in a blender or with electric mixer. Add remaining port wine or the reserved prune juice to keep the prunes moist. Whip the cream and mix half with the prunes. Sweeten remaining cream with confectioner's sugar and use as a garnish. Sprinkle top with almonds.
Yields 4 servings.

☆ ☆

For information about
Lee & Associates, Inc.
Marketing, Public Relations, Advertising
Contact them at:
145 S. Fairfax Ave., Suite 301
Los Angeles, CA 90036
phone: (323) 938-3300
email: leepr@aol.com
website: www.leeassociates-mkt.com

☆ ☆

Look for Leo Pearlstein's latest book, "Recipes of the Stars."

He shares many favorite recipes from Stars, past and present— including appetizers, side dishes, entrees and desserts.

Easy-to-prepare classic recipes range from Bob Hope's "Crunchy Broiled Grapefruit" and Mickey Rooney's "Kahlua Savory Stuffing" to Phyllis Diller's "Dill-Stuffed Sole" and Dinah Shore's "Prune Whip and Port Wine."

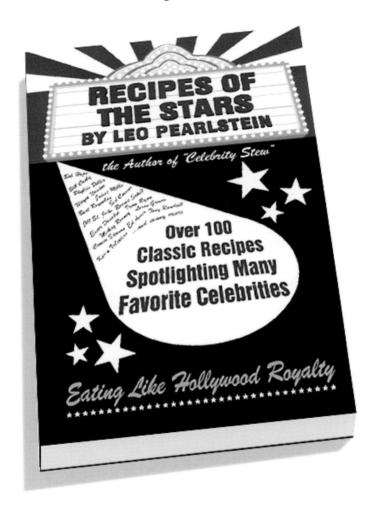

Published By

HOLLYWOOD CIRCLE PRESS

☆ ☆

☆ ☆

Give The Gift of "Celebrity Stew" or "Recipes of the Stars" to Your Friends and Colleagues

Check Your Local Bookstore, Online Bookseller or Order Here

YES, I want _____ copy(s) of "Celebrity Stew" Hardcover, (ISBN 0-9711306-1-4) for **$32.95** each.

YES, I want _____ copy(s) of "Celebrity Stew" Softcover, (ISBN 0-9711306-1-2) for **$22.95** each.

YES, I want _____ copy(s) of "Recipes of the Stars" Softcover, (ISBN 0-9711306-2-0) (Reg. Retail Price is $14.95).
Special Price with this order form, only **$12.95**

Include $3.95 shipping and handling for one book, and $1.95 for each additional book.

California residents must include applicable sales tax: $2.72 for each Hardcover, and $1.89 for each Softcover.

International orders, please contact publisher.

Payment must accompany orders. Allow 2 - 4 weeks for delivery.

My check or money order for $_____ is enclosed
Please charge my ☐Visa ☐MasterCard ☐American Express

Name _____

Address _____

City/State/Zip _____

Phone (   ) _____Email _____

Card # _____

Exp. Date _____Signature _____

or Call Toll Free: 866-789-BOOK
(2665)

Make your check payable and return to:
HOLLYWOOD CIRCLE PRESS
P.O. Box 48051
Los Angeles, CA 90048
Visit Our Website: www.celebritystew.com

☆ ☆

Index

☆ ☆

Page numbers in parenthesized italics indicate photos; all other page numbers indicate text.

☆ ☆